TOP 10 STOCKHOLM

PAUL EADE

EYEWITNESS TRAVEL

Left **Outdoor café, Sergels Torg** Right **Södermalm's north shoreline**

LONDON, NEW YORK,
MELBOURNE, MUNICH AND DELHI
www.dk.com

Printed and bound in China by
South China Printing Co. Ltd.

First American Edition, 2013
13 14 15 16 10 9 8 7 6 5 4 3 2 1

Published in the United States by
Dorling Kindersley Limited
80 Strand
London WC2R 0RL, UK

Floors are referred to throughout in accordance with European usage; i.e. the "first floor" is the floor above ground level.

ISSN 1479-344X
ISBN 978 0 7566 9231 5

A catalogue record for this book is available from the Library of Congress.

Within each Top 10 list in this book, no hierarchy of quality or popularity is implied. All 10 are, in the editor's opinion, of roughly equal merit.

Contents

Stockholm's Top 10

The information in this DK Eyewitness Top 10 Travel Guide is checked regularly.

Every effort has been made to ensure that this book is as up-to-date as possible at the time of going to press. Some details, however, such as telephone numbers, opening hours, prices, gallery hanging arrangements and travel information are liable to change. The publishers cannot accept responsibility for any consequences arising from the use of this book, nor for any material on third party websites, and cannot guarantee that any website address in this book will be a suitable source of travel information. We value the views and suggestions of our readers very highly. Please write to: Publisher, DK Eyewitness Travel Guides, Dorling Kindersley, 80 Strand, London WC2R 0RL, or email: travelguides@dk.com

Cover: Front – **Alamy Images**: Frank Chmura main; **Dorling Kindersley**: James Tye bl.
Spine – **Dorling Kindersley**: James Tye b. Back – **Dorling Kindersley**: James Tye tl, tc, tr.

Left **Swedish folk art, Nordiska Museet** Right **Façade of Naturhistoriska Riksmuseet**

Left **Statue of naturalist Carl Linneaus in Humlegården** Right **Stained-glass window, Storkyrkan**

Key to abbreviations
Adm *admission charge* **kr** *kronor*

STOCKHOLM'S TOP10

TOP 10 Stockholm's Highlights

A city of contrasts dictated by the weather, Stockholm can offer Christmas card scenes in winter and sundrenched quaysides and waterways in summer. Unique museums and cool nightlife make it a year-round destination but wrap up for the harsh winter months. No one would ever pretend that Stockholm is cheap to visit, but there are bargains for those in the know and museums, attractions and transport are all very reasonably priced.

1 Skansen

Part re-creation of Swedish traditional life, part zoo and part children's fair, Skansen's hilly park has something for everyone, with surprises around every corner. Put aside at least a half day to make the most of it *(see pp8–9)*.

2 Vasamuseet

Lifted from the sea bed in 1961, the *Vasa* warship emerged after 333 years in remarkably good condition. Get up close to the vessel, which sank in Stockholm harbour on its maiden voyage *(see pp10–11)*.

Norrmalm
KUNGSGATAN
VASAGATAN
KLARABERGSVIADUKTEN
City
Klara Sjö
NORR MÄLARSTRAND
4
Riddarfjärden

3 Stockholm Archipelago

An entire summer would not be enough to explore the archipelago's gems – beaches, forests and seaside restaurants. Go camping, or just relax and take in its beauty from a steamship *(see pp12–15)*.

4 Stadshuset

The City Hall belies its stark and imposing exterior with magnificent halls, including the Prince's Gallery. The tower offers stunning views *(see pp16–17)*.

5 Drottningholm

Home to the Swedish royal family, this UNESCO World Heritage Site takes visitors back to 17th- and 18th-century grandeur. The extensive, free-to-visit gardens are a delight *(see pp18–19)*.

Preceding pages **Queen Hedvig Eleonora's State Bedroom, Drottningholm Palace**

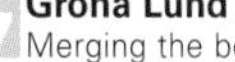

7 Gröna Lund

Merging the best traditions of fairgrounds with the latest hair-raising rides, Gröna Lund has something for all ages and tastes – from the 19th-century carousel and sideshows to free-fall towers *(see pp22–3)*.

6 The Royal Palace (Kungliga Slottet)

Built over 63 years after its predecessor burnt down in 1697, the Royal Palace is an extravagant combination of Italian, French and Swedish influences. Although no longer a royal residence, it still hosts many state functions *(see pp20–21)*.

8 Nordiska Museet

Experience the Swedish way of life from the 16th to the 21st centuries in this museum, home to over one and a half million exhibits – from jewellery and Strindberg's paintings to everyday items from typical homes through the ages *(see pp24–5)*.

10 Hagaparken

A green oasis on the city's northern edge, this "English park" reveals its secrets along winding, wooded paths *(see pp28–9)*.

9 Historiska Museet

Opened in 1943, this museum made its name with exhibits from the Viking era, as well as its exceptionally good collections from the early Middle Ages. The Guldrummet (Gold Room) is one of Stockholm's most remarkable sights *(see pp26–7)*.

Skansen

This open-air museum, essentially a journey of Sweden through the ages, was founded in 1891. It contains over 150 traditional buildings from around the country, dating from the 14th to the early 20th century – dismantled, transported and rebuilt on site. It is also home to Nordic wild animals in a natural habitat, and trees and plants from all parts of Sweden. Skansen changes naturally with the seasons – bustling and lively in summer, calm and serene in winter – but it is so vast that it is easy to find a quiet spot.

Electric car for kids near Bredablick Tower

Admission prices vary throughout the year and are significantly cheaper in winter. They are at their highest in summer and during special events. Check Skansen's website for details.

Skansen Terrassen, open all year round, offers good-value meals, with a dish of the day, including a vegetarian option, an à la carte menu and children's dishes.

- *Map F4*
- *Djurgårdsslätten 49–51*
- *08 442 80 00*
- *Tram 7; Bus 44; Ferry from Slussen to Djurgården.*
- *Open 10am onwards daily; check website for details about closing timings during the year.*
- *Adm: 100–150 kr (adults); 60 kr (6–15s); under 5s free. Aquarium: 100 kr (adults); 60 kr (6–15s); under 5s free. Prices depend on season and events.*
- *www.skansen.se/en*

Top 10 Features

1. Nordic Animals
2. Historical Buildings
3. Skansen Glassworks
4. Gardens
5. Funicular Railway
6. Galejan Fairground
7. Aquarium
8. Bredablick Tower
9. Lill-Skansen
10. Cafés and Restaurants

1 Nordic Animals

The lynx, brown bear *(above)*, wolf and moose enjoy a roomy natural habitat on the park's northern cliffs, while Swedish sheep, goats and pigs live around the farmsteads. Wild birds that have made Skansen their home include the grey heron and barnacle goose.

2 Historical Buildings

In the 19th-century town quarter, staff in traditional attire bake bread or make pottery. There are many farmsteads, churches and halls; several are open to public *(main image)*.

3 Skansen Glassworks

Highly skilled glass-blowers use traditional tools to create crystal in designs *(above)* unique to Skansen. Their wares can be bought on site.

Travel to Skansen on the vintage tram from Norrmalmstorg – it stops right outside Skansen's main entrance.

4 Gardens

Gardens *(above)* and cultivated patches are designed to provide a contextual landscape to the buildings. The Skåne farmstead has a shady garden in keeping with rural southern Sweden, while the town quarters include allotments and herb plots.

5 Funicular Railway

The mountain railway, Skansen's Bergbana *(right)*, was built in 1897. Cable operated, it starts at the Hazelius entrance and is perfect for visitors with prams or wheelchairs, or those simply wanting to enjoy a ride.

6 Galejan Fairground

Enjoy the vintage hand-painted carousels *(above)* and traditional sideshows. Kids will love activities such as fishing for ducks.

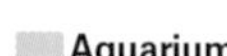

7 Aquarium

Housed in the aquarium are 200 exotic species as well as the World of Monkeys. Walk among lemurs and admire baboons and crocodiles.

8 Bredablick Tower

This 30-m (98-ft) high brick tower *(left)*, is located in the north-eastern part of Skansen. The hill, on which it is built, rises 45 m (148 ft) above sea level. Kids will love a ride in the colourful electric cars near the tower.

9 Lill-Skansen

A firm favourite since 1955, the children's zoo offers kids an opportunity to pet cats, goats, guinea pigs, rabbits or even a Greek tortoise.

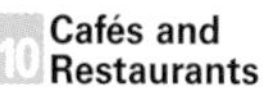

10 Cafés and Restaurants

Have a romantic dinner at the Tre Byttor Tavern or savour a classic Swedish *smörgåsbord* at Solliden. Cafés and kiosks serve snacks, waffles and cakes. Many bring their own picnic to enjoy outdoors, or inside Solliden.

Special Events

Sweden's major festivals are celebrated here – Midsummer, the traditional Christmas market, and New Year's Eve fireworks. Sing-a-long in Skansen is a Swedish institution featuring contemporary artists. It is held on Tuesday evenings in summer and broadcast on TV as well.

A handy free map of Skansen is included in the admission price.

TOP 10 Vasamuseet

An impressive warship built between 1626 and 1628, the Vasa *had a fatal flaw – she was top heavy with insufficient ballast. She capsized and sank on her maiden voyage, shortly after setting sail. In 1961, her remarkably intact hull was raised after 333 years under water. She is now preserved under very carefully controlled conditions to prevent decay, along with a host of fascinating artifacts recovered during the salvage operation. The museum also tells the story of the* Vasa *and her recovery. Models and reconstructions bring it all to life, while getting up close to the vessel is a unique experience.*

Scale model of the Vasa

The museum has information sheets in 15 different languages, including English, German, Spanish and French.

A café serves both light refreshments and hot and cold food.

- *Map Q4*
- *Galärvarvsvägen 14*
- *08 519 548 00*
- *Tram 7; Bus 44 to Nordiska Museet/ Vasamuseet; Ferry from Slussen to Djurgården.*
- *Open Jun–end-Aug: 8:30am–6pm daily; Sep–end-May: 10am–5pm daily (till 8pm Wed), closed 1 Jan and 23–25 Dec.*
- *Adm: 130 kr (adults); 100 kr (students with valid student ID); under 19s free. The museum is closed for six weeks in spring 2013.*
- *www.vasamuseet.se/en*

Top 10 Features

1. Stern
2. Lion Figurehead
3. Upper Deck
4. Skeletons
5. The Salvaging Exhibition
6. Sculptures
7. Gun Deck
8. Cannons
9. Objects
10. The Vasa Garden

1 Stern

Many of the ship's 500 sculptures were centred on the magnificent stern, a symbol of Sweden's might. Although it was badly damaged, it has been painstakingly restored to reveal the ostentatious ornamentation *(below)*.

2 Lion Figurehead

Many lion sculptures reflect the fact that King Gustav II Adolf, who commissioned the vessel, was known as the Lion of the North. The crowning glory is the 3-m (10-ft) long lion figurehead *(below)*.

3 Upper Deck

Carpenters restored the destroyed upper deck in the 1990s. While new parts were needed to complete it, original timber has been used as much as possible.

4 Skeletons

Around 15 skeletons were found during the salvage operation. The exhibition Face to Face includes a fantasy "meeting" with some of the individuals from the *Vasa* in a film, and through six facial reconstructions.

The museum is fun for children, with its models, reconstructions and experiments.

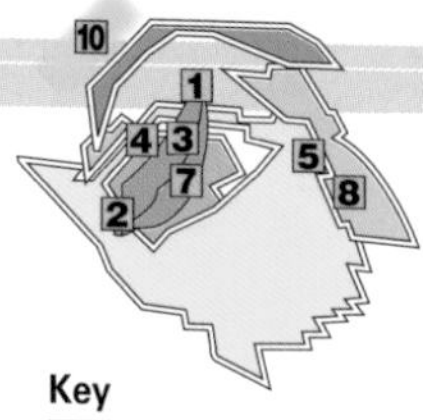

Key

- Ground Floor
- Second Floor
- Third Floor
- Fourth Floor

5 The Salvaging Exhibition

Raising the *Vasa* took over a year and a half from the first experimental lift in 1959 to 24 April 1961, when *Vasa's* emergence to the surface was shown live on TV. This exhibit documents the operation from discovery through to the final lifting and transportation.

6 Sculptures

Several sculptures on the warship, including one of cherubs around the royal emblem *(above)*, show how King Gustav II Adolf wanted the world to see himself and Sweden.

7 Gun Deck

The *Vasa* was armed with powerful artillery; there were 11 kg (24 lb) cast-iron guns on both its upper *(above)* and lower gun decks. Enter its full-size copy and experience life aboard a ship.

8 Cannons

Most of the 64 cannons were salvaged in the 17th century, using diving bells for the recovery operation. The museum displays three of the largest *(below)*, cast in bronze and weighing 11 kg (24 lbs) each.

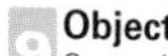

9 Objects

Several objects were recovered from the ship and sea bed. The upper gun deck alone yielded a chest of personal items – a felt hat, sewing tools, a comb, pewter tankards *(below)*, gloves, a drinks keg, a wooden spoon, several coins and some smaller belongings.

10 The Vasa Garden

The garden cultivates plants that would have been vital to the health of those aboard, for example rambling hops, harvested in late summer to flavour and conserve the ship's beer.

The Sinking

On 10 August 1628, the *Vasa* sat ready for sea, moored below the Royal Palace. For the first few hundred metres (several hundred feet), she was pulled along using anchors. As the *Vasa* began to move on her own, four of her 10 sails were set. As soon as she caught the wind, she heeled over twice. Water rushed in through the open gunports and she sank after sailing barely 1,300 m (4,265 ft). Around 30 of an estimated 150 people on board died. The *Vasa* sank because of insufficient ballast to balance the cannons and rigging; this caused the hull to ride too high over the water.

The Vasamuseet is wheelchair accessible.

TOP 10 Stockholm Archipelago

Stretching from a few metres outside Stockholm to 60 km (37 miles) further east, the Stockholm Archipelago (Skärgard) is one of the most spectacular in the world. Consisting of around 30,000 islands and islets, it changes in character further east towards the open sea. Around 150 islands are inhabited; others are little more than bare rock. The archipelago comes alive in summer, when it is possible to take anything from a 25-minute boat hop to Fjäderholmarna to a two-hour plus journey much further afield. The islands have inspired several writers and painters alike.

House on one of the archipelago islands

Transport to many of the islands is very limited, sometimes to one boat a day. All the islands are accessible by scheduled boat services, but plan your trip carefully.

Facilities on the islands range from top-quality restaurants in the more popular destinations to simple cafés or kiosks or in some instances, nothing at all.

- *Ferry from Stockholm to the archipelago: Waxholmsbolaget*
- *08 614 64 50*
- *www.waxholmsbolaget.se*

Top 10 Islands

1. Siaröfortet
2. Norröra
3. Fjäderholmarna
4. Arholma
5. Finnhamn
6. Ängsö National Park
7. Sandhamn
8. Vaxholm
9. Grinda
10. Utö

1 Siaröfortet

Built as part of a defence line against naval forces, Siaröfortet is a warren of underground rooms, including barracks and a kitchen, plus guns embedded in the rock. It was decommissioned in the 1960s and has now been restored as a museum.

2 Norröra

The inspiration and film set for Astrid Lindgren's TV series *Life on Seacrow Island*, Norröra has changed little since the series was made in 1964. It has a cafe and nature walks.

3 Fjäderholmarna

An ideal day trip for those who want a taste of the archipelago without a long journey, this island can be reached from May to October by frequent boats from Nybroplan or Slussen. Despite being popular, the island also has secluded picnic spots.

4 Arholma

The last outpost in the northern archipelago, Arholma has a beautiful landscape, much of which is a nature reserve. Sights include a Midsummer pole in the form of a fully rigged mast and the Arholma watch beacon *(above)*, built in 1768, now used as an art and crafts store.

Boat schedules may change in winter if the ice is very thick.

5 Finnhamn

A group of islands in the outer archipelago, Finnhamn is accessible by boat all year round and its hostel welcomes guests *(left)* from late-spring till autumn. It also has an organic farm.

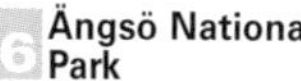

6 Ängsö National Park

A national park since 1909, this is the place to experience a real-life slice of old Sweden, with pastures much as they were hundreds of years ago. There is a signposted network of walking trails.

7 Sandhamn

The archipelago's yachting centre, Sandhamn's harbour is busy in summer and this is reflected in its lively party atmosphere. However, it also has a superb long beach, Trouville, which is perfect for families.

8 Vaxholm

The main archipelago town, with about 10,000 people, Vaxholm *(left)* has several restaurants and cafés along the waterfront, where frequent boats arrive. The island is also accessible by Bus 670 from Stockholm.

9 Grinda

One of the most popular archipelago destinations, Grinda offers a range of accommodation *(right)*. The island's restaurants are highly popular in summer.

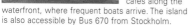

10 Utö

In the outer part of the archipelago, Utö *(left)* offers activities such as canoeing and cycling. It has pretty beaches, good lodging options and cafés.

Some More Islands

Gällnö, a long-standing agricultural community, has striking landscapes of fields, meadows and glacial rocks. **Själbottna**, part of the Östra Lagnö nature reserve, is an excellent place to pitch a tent for the night and has secluded spots for bathing. **Landsort**, on the southernmost outpost of Öja, has Sweden's oldest functioning lighthouse. **Rödlöga**, meaning "bathed in red", is a wild, granite island on the outer reaches of the archipelago, the last port of call for regular boat services.

The round semaphore sign on jetties must be placed in a vertical position to tell the captain you are waiting to board a boat.

Left **Sailboats cruising the archipelago** Right **Camping on one of the islands**

Things to Do on the Islands

1 Steamboat Tours

Beautifully maintained veteran steamboats operate in high summer. Take one of the scheduled services for a day trip to Vaxholm or to one of the other islands such as Grinda. Alternatively, choose a day or evening cruise with the option of lunch or dinner, sometimes with a jazz band.

2 Farming

Stay overnight at Östanvik Gård, a thriving archipelago farm, on the island of Nämdö, which dates back to the 16th century, or buy produce directly from its little shop. *www.ostanviksgard.se*

3 Cottage Rentals

Experience island life at close quarters by renting a cottage either for a weekend or holiday. Some islands have limited shopping facilities and often no alcohol store, so you may need to bring most or all your supplies with you. Destination Stockholms Skärgård has cottages to rent in the archipelago. *www.dess.se*

4 Winter Boat Trips

Enjoy the tranquility of the archipelago amidst snow and ice with a winter cruise. Strömma offers a three-hour brunch cruise, every Saturday and Sunday, aboard the 70-year-old *S/S Stockholm*. *www.strömma.se*

5 Day Trip with Lunch at an Archipelago Restaurant

Numerous day trip packages take away the hassle of organizing travel and food, especially as tables in many restaurants can be fully booked in the high season. Visit the website for a choice of day trips. *www.visitskargarden.se*

Crayfish buffet

6 Camping

With the right of public access, anyone can pitch a tent in most open spaces. However, if you want fresh water and toilets, there are many designated camping spots on several islands, either free of charge, or for a small fee.

7 Boat Hiking

The boat hiker's pass, for 420 kr, is valid for five days from the first journey and can be used on all Waxholmsbolaget boats.

Waterfront cottage in an archipelago island

All of the larger archipelago boats offer some sort of refreshment facility – usually a kiosk with drinks and simple snacks.

Kayaking
Paddling in the archipelago is a good way to get close to the smaller islands and wildlife; trip length depends on wind, weather and experience.

Getting There and Around

Boat timetables are available in printed form from all SL (see p106) travel offices and from tourist centres. Schedules can be complicated – some boats only sail on certain days – so check carefully and, if you are taking a day trip, make sure you can get back. The fastest are the Cinderella ships, which notably cut journey times to the middle and outer archipelago. You can also reach a lot of islands by bus, followed by a shorter boat trip – connections are given in the timetable. Winter schedules are limited. The main boat operator is Waxholmsbolaget – its website, in Swedish and English, contains timetables and journey planners.

Passengers waiting at the quayside to board steamships

The pass comes with a map and suggested itineraries, including where to arrive at an island, hike across it and leave by ferry to continue on to another island. *www.waxholmsbolaget.se/visitor/archipelago-traffic/good-to-know*

8 Beaches and Swimming

The water might be quite chilly but swimming and paddling are immensely popular in summer. The ever-popular Grinda is about an hour by ferry from Stockholm, or simply take Bus 428X to Björkvik for swimming and sands with fine views across the water.

9 Kayaking

At Ingmarsö visitors can rent single or double kayaks, or take a group tour with a guide. The boat trip from Stockholm to Ingmarsö takes two and a half hours to the south jetty. *www.ingmarsokajak.se*

10 Fishing

Fishing with a hand tackle is allowed everywhere in the archipelago. For serious fishing, hire a guide, many of whom offer boats, equipment, life vests and overalls. There are organized fishing trips from time to time – check at the tourist offices for more details.

Strömkajen, in Stockholm, outside the Grand Hotel, is Waxholmsbolaget's main departure point.

TOP 10 Stadshuset

The imposing red-brick City Hall is one of Stockholm's major landmarks, dominating the northern shore of the bay of Riddarfjärden. Completed in 1923, it is built in the National Romantic style, with the austere Nordic Gothic building juxtaposed with northern Italian features. Today, it contains offices for around 200 local politicians and civil servants, and hosts the annual Nobel Prize Banquet. The interior can be viewed by guided tour only, but visitors can stroll at leisure through the courtyard and gardens, as well as climb the tower for a small fee. A cafeteria serves classic Swedish dishes at lunchtime.

Fresco in the Blue Hall

For photos of Stadshuset, walk eastwards to the path on the central railway bridge, Centralbron. From there, you can click great photos from across the water.

Adjacent to the hall, towards Norr Mälarstrand, a kiosk sells ice creams and hot and cold drinks.

- *Map K4*
- *Hantverkargatan 1*
- *08 508 29 058*
- *Buses 3 and 62 stop directly outside Stadshuset.*
- *Groups of more than 10 require reservations.*
- *www.stockholm.se/CityHall*
- *Stadshuskallaren: www.restofair.se/home-en*

Top 10 Features

1. Tower
2. Three Crowns
3. The Golden Hall
4. Prince's Gallery
5. The Blue Hall
6. The Oval Room
7. Gardens
8. Statues
9. Council Chamber
10. Cellar Restaurant

1 Tower

Climb to the top of the 106-m (348-ft) tall tower for superb views over the Old Town and City from the open-air terrace. Visit the Tower Museum, located in the middle of the tower. A lift goes half-way to the top.

2 Three Crowns

Sweden's heraldic symbol of the three gold crowns – Tre Kronor – tops the tower *(right)*.

3 The Golden Hall

More than 18 million glass and gold mosaic fragments, the work of artist Einar Forseth (1892–1988), adorn the Golden Hall's walls. They depict Swedish history using a Byzantine-inspired style.

4 Prince's Gallery

On the south side of Stadshuset are French windows offering a wonderful view of Lake Mälaren and Södermalm; the gallery's opposite wall *(left)* reflects this in a fresco called *Stockholm's Shores* (1922). This along with another fresco, *The City on the Water*, was painted by Prince Eugen who was an artist and the brother of the Swedish King Gustav V.

The City Hall shop is open from 8:30am–4:30pm daily.

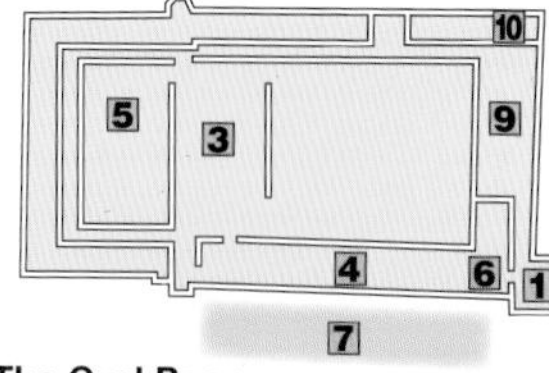

5 The Blue Hall

The venue for the Nobel Prize Banquet, the Blue Hall was meant to have its bricks painted blue, but architect Ragnar Östberg was so taken with the natural red that he had a last-minute change of heart. However, the name remained.

6 The Oval Room

Weddings and civil partnerships are solemnized in the Oval Room. The walls are covered with a series of five 300 year-old tapestries woven in Beauvais in France.

7 Gardens

The south-facing garden *(above)*, popular with sightseers and sunbathers, sits between Lake Mälaren and Stadshuset.

8 Statues

The gardens have many statues. The steps to the water are flanked by two of Carl Eldh's sculptures: *The Song* and *The Dance*. On a 20-m (65-ft) pillar in the southeast corner is *Engelbrekt the Freedom Fighter* by Christian Eriksson.

9 Council Chamber

Stockholm's local councillors meet in this magnificent chamber *(above)* every third Monday. The 19-m (62-ft) high ceiling takes inspiration from the Swedish Viking Age. The public gallery can accomodate about 200 spectators.

10 Cellar Restaurant

Dine in Stadshuskällaren, the cellar restaurant *(above)*. It offers a wide range of classic Swedish dishes such as meatballs or marinated salmon.

Guided Tours

The interior of the City Hall can only be visited by guided tour, available both in Swedish and English, but they may be cancelled due to events in the building. Tours in English, are conducted daily every hour from 10am to 3pm all year round, and more frequently in June, July and August – every 30 minutes from 9:30am to 4pm. The 45-minute guided tour goes through the official part of the City Hall from a historical, architectural and cultural point of view. Tours need not be booked in advance.

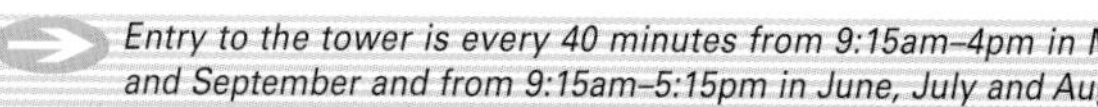

Entry to the tower is every 40 minutes from 9:15am–4pm in May and September and from 9:15am–5:15pm in June, July and August.

Top 10 Drottningholm

The superbly preserved Drottningholm Palace and its grounds date from the 17th and 18th centuries, inspired by French models such as Versailles. On UNESCO's World Heritage list since 1991, the palace is the royal family's permanent home. Rooms in the southern wing are reserved for this purpose; the rest of the palace and grounds are open to the public. The grounds have trees dating from the palace's heyday as a royal court. It fell into decay and was abandoned in the mid-19th century, but after a six-year long renovation from 1907, it began to be reused by the royal court.

Studio of Evert Lundquist near the Chinese Pavilion

Drottningholm is a great day out for budget travellers – the gardens and Guards' Tent are all free – more than enough for an afternoon's visit.

The visitor's centre provides information and sells tickets to the sights. There is also a gift shop and restaurant.

- *Map G2*
- *08 402 62 80*
- *Ferry from Stockholm : www.stromma.se*
- *Palace: Open 14 Jan–31 Mar: noon–3:30pm Sat & Sun; Apr & Oct: 11am–3:30pm Fri–Sun; May–Aug: 10am–4:30pm daily; Sep: 11am–3:30pm daily; Nov– 9 Dec: noon–3:30pm Sat & Sun; 31 Dec–8 Jan: noon–3:30pm daily; closed 12–30 Dec.*
- *Adm: 100 kr (adults); 50 kr (7–18s & students). Combination ticket includes the Chinese Pavilion: 145 kr (adults), 75 kr (7–18s & students).*
- *www.kungahuset.se*

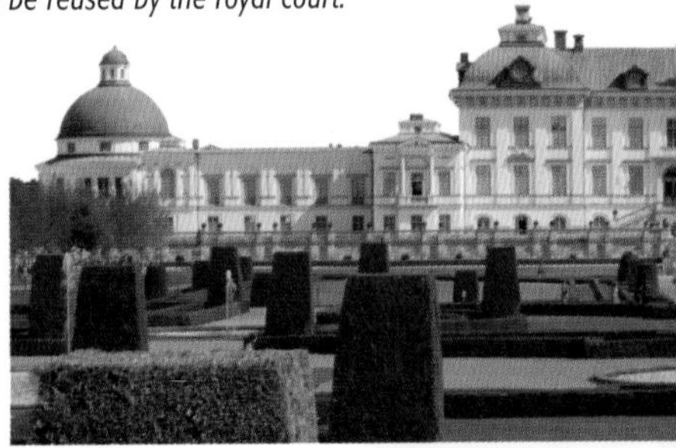

Top 10 Features

1. The Staircase
2. Queen Hedvig Eleonora's State Bedroom
3. Queen Lovisa Ulrika's Library
4. Chinese Pavilion
5. The Nature Path
6. Court Theatre
7. Baroque Garden
8. The Studio of Evert Lundquist
9. Guards' Tent
10. Drottningholm by Boat

1 The Staircase

Large statues of nine muses are placed on the balustrade *(above)* and *trompe-l'oeil* paintings by Johan Sylvius adorn the walls of the stair hall.

2 Queen Hedvig Eleonora's State Bedroom

Created over 15 years, the queen's state bedroom *(above)* was the heart of the state reception suite in the 17th century.

3 Queen Lovisa Ulrika's Library

Decorated in the 18th century by Jean Eric Rehn for the queen, the library *(below)* includes paintings of historic events such as the crossing of the Great Belt in Denmark in 1658.

Taking photos or filming with cameras or mobiles is not allowed inside the palace; mobiles must be turned off.

4 Chinese Pavilion

At the time when this pavilion *(right)* was built, as a surprise gift from King Adolf Fredrik to his wife Lovisa Ulrika in 1753, there was great interest in all things Chinese – the style is what was considered to be typically Chinese 250 years ago.

5 The Nature Path

Close to the Chinese Pavilion, the nature path is a peaceful walk for anyone who wants to learn more about the flora and fauna and cultural history linked to the island of Lovön where Drottningholm is situated. The path is also signposted in Braille.

7 Baroque Garden

The oldest part of the gardens *(main image)* is laid out in a formal French style. Many of the statues here were taken from cities captured by the Swedish army, including the Wallenstein Palace in Prague.

6 Court Theatre

The world's oldest theatre *(left)*, still preserved in its original condition, dates from 1766. Each summer it hosts around 30 performances, mainly 18th-century opera and ballet.

9 Guards' Tent

Built in 1781 to serve as quarters for the dragoons of Gustav III, the Guards' Tent *(above)* is built to resemble a tent in a Turkish army camp. The history of Drottningholm's Royal Guard is described in one of the rooms.

8 The Studio of Evert Lundquist

The studio is a museum housing oil paintings, charcoal drawings and dry-point engravings by Evert Lundquist (1904–1994).

10 Drottningholm by Boat

From May to October steamships *(above)* cruise on Lake Mälaren from Stockholm to the palace. Boats leave from Stadshusbron, right beside the City Hall. Visit the website for departures and fares.

Getting to Drottningholm

Take the underground green line to Brommaplan, then change to Bus 301 or 323 for Drottningholm. Alternatively, Buses 177 and 178 go to Drottningholm from Mörby and Solna stations. You can also take the Nockebybanan tram from Alvik, on the green line, to Nockeby, and walk for over a kilometre (a mile) to Drottningholm. Cyclists can follow the path from the centre of Stockholm to Drottningholm.

Umbrellas, large bags and backpacks must be checked into the palace cloakroom during the visit.

The Royal Palace (Kungliga Slottet)

Stunning rooms – 1,430 of them – and priceless jewels and artifacts are just some of the highlights of the 250-year-old Royal Palace. As one of the largest royal palaces still in use – it is the workplace of the monarchy and used for most of its official receptions – this is deservedly one of the city's showpiece attractions. Reminiscent of a Roman Baroque palazzo, it was designed by architect Nicodemus Tessin to replace the old Tre Kronor castle that burnt down in 1697. Containing five different museums, the palace is guarded by the Royal Guards.

Carving inside the Royal Chapel

The entry fee to the palace includes a 45-minute guided tour. There are tours in Swedish, English and German year round.

There are many cafés and restaurants in the surrounding Old Town area.

- *Map M4*
- *Slottsbacken, Gamla Stan*
- *08 402 61 30 (weekdays 9am–noon)*
- *Underground: Gamla Stan, Kungsträdgården; Buses 2, 43, 55, 71, 76*
- *Open 15 May–16 Sep: 10am–5pm daily; 17 Sep–14 May: noon–4pm Tue–Sun*
- *Royal Apartments: 150 kr (adults); 75 kr (7–18s & students); under 7s free. For details regarding visiting the different museums check the website.*
- *www.kungahuset.se*

Top 10 Features

1. Royal Chapel
2. The Guest Apartments
3. The State Apartments
4. Gustav III's Museum of Antiquities
5. The Hall of State
6. The Bernadotte Apartments
7. The Royal Guard
8. Tre Kronor Museum
9. Karl XI's Gallery
10. The Treasury

1 Royal Chapel

The richly decorated chapel *(main image)* holds mass for employees of the Royal Court every Sunday; all are welcome to attend. It also holds organ and classical music concerts.

2 The Guest Apartments

This treasure trove of beautiful rooms includes the Meleager Salon, a mix of Rococo and Gustavian styles. There is also a cabinet piano in mahogany with pilasters made of white marble.

3 The State Apartments

The royal family has lived at Drottningholm *(see pp18–19)* since 1982, but earlier inhabitants have left their mark here. Gustav III's state bedchamber and the White Sea Hall *(left)* epitomize the height of 18th-century elegance.

The Royal Apartments may close in conjunction with the Royal Palace's official duties. Check the website for details.

4 Gustav III's Museum of Antiquities

First opened in 1794, this museum *(above)* includes a collection of antique statues bought by King Gustav III on a visit to Italy (1783–4).

10 The Treasury

The state regalia, including King Erik XIV's crown *(below)*, are kept in deep cellar vaults at the bottom of 56 well-worn steps. The silver baptismal font from 1696 is still used at royal baptisms.

5 The Hall of State

The highlight of the royal apartments, the Hall of State features the silver throne of Queen Kristina, who became queen at the age of just six, before abdicating at the age of 21 to convert to Catholicism.

7 The Royal Guard

Drawn from the Swedish armed forces, the Royal Guard *(above)* has been protecting the palace since 1523. The changing of the guard takes place daily at midday, sometimes with music.

8 Tre Kronor Museum

Built around the remains of a 12th-century defensive wall and housed in vaults from the 16th and 17th centuries, this museum takes visitors back to the original Tre Kronor palace, most of which was destroyed in a fire in 1697.

9 Karl XI's Gallery

This magnificent room *(above)* is the palace's banqueting hall; official dinners, state dinners and a dinner in honour of the Nobel Prize winners are all held here.

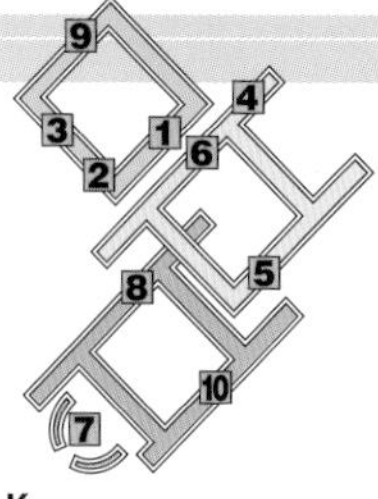

Key

- Ground Floor
- First Floor
- Second Floor

6 The Bernadotte Apartments

The king receives foreign dignitaries in the East Octagonal Cabinet – the rooms are as they were in the mid-18th century. Do not miss Queen Lovisa Ulrika's audience chamber *(below)*.

Palace History

Kungliga Slottet originated as a 13th-century fortress, but evolved into a palace in the 16th century. Work to develop it began in 1692 under the direction of architect Nicodemus Tessin the Younger, but in 1697, a fire destroyed most of the palace, except the north wing. Tessin submitted drawings for the new palace to the Swedish government – the plan was for it to be built in about five years. However, the royal family was not able to move back in until 1754.

The Treasury, the Tre Kronor Museum and Gustav III's Museum of Antiquities are not affected by the closure of the Royal Apartments.

Top 10 Gröna Lund

Founded in 1883, Gröna Lund, or Green Grove, is Sweden's oldest amusement park – a mix of modern thrills and old-fashioned charm in an excellent waterside setting. Suitable for all ages, it boasts a wide range of rides and attractions. The latest of seven roller coasters was installed in 2011, but there are also more sedate rides – carousels with original fittings from the 19th century and traditional sideshows. Gröna Lund is also a major concert venue – The Who played here in 1966, Bob Marley attracted a record audience of 32,000 in 1980 and Lady Gaga was on stage in 2009.

Flying elephant in Gröna Lund

Euros (notes only) are accepted at all the entrance and ticket booths, souvenir and photo shops, as well as kiosks and stands. The highest note accepted is €50 and change is given in kronor – the service centre exchanges euros for kronor. There is one ATM in the park by the Free Fall Towers and one just outside the main entrance.

Kaskad is a family restaurant located by the waterfront. It serves meat and fish dishes, pizza, salads and pasta and operates during park opening hours. The Tyrol restaurant has an outdoor area and offers upmarket food.

- *Map R6*
- *Lilla Allmänna gränd 9*
- *08 587 501 00*
- *Tram 7; Bus 44; Ferry from Slussen to Djurgården.*
- *Open Apr–Sep, check website calendar for full details as opening times vary according to the time of year.*
- *www.gronalund.com*

Top 10 Features

1. Roller Coasters
2. Flying Carpet
3. Fun House
4. Tunnel of Love
5. The Old Carousel
6. Mirror Pavilion
7. Stages
8. Restaurants and Bars
9. Free Fall Towers
10. Haunted House

1 Roller Coasters

There are seven roller coasters, including the Jetline, which reach speeds of 90 km (56 miles) per hour, and the new wooden Twister *(above)* by the waterfront. The Ladybird can be enjoyed by all ages.

2 Flying Carpet

A wild and scary ride is what you would expect from a real flying carpet and this does not disappoint. Sit on the edge for a thrilling ride.

3 Fun House

Lustiga Huset, or Fun House, is a genuine original from the 1920s, and has been the inspiration and design for several fun houses in the world. It has wacky rooms, wobbly bridges and flying carpets.

4 Tunnel of Love

This tunnel takes you through a magical fairytale world decked with twinkling lights. Hold hands, steal a kiss or just enjoy its charm *(left)*.

Check the website for the admission fee on the date you plan to visit. You need to buy coupons for the rides and attractions.

5 The Old Carousel

The German-built carousel *(above)* dates from 1892. Choose from riding lovable pigs, proud lions, traditional white horses or even a giraffe.

6 Mirror Pavilion

Pull silly faces and transform into absurd shapes in this temple of laughter, dating from the 1930s.

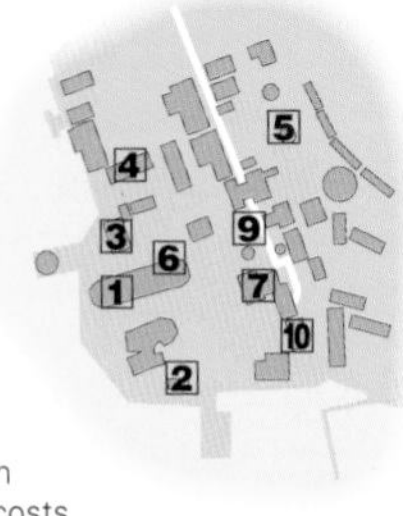

7 Stages

There is both a large and small stage at Gröna Lund. Some concerts are included in an ordinary day ticket, but it costs more for major events. A *Gröna Kortet* or green card for 199 kr provides unlimited admission, including to concerts, over a calendar year.

8 Restaurants and Bars

There are five restaurants and bars *(above)* plus kiosks selling traditional Swedish waffles and ice cream. Other outlets specialize in Thai and Mexican food, kebabs, falafel and burgers.

9 Free Fall Towers

This ride is for intense thrill seekers only, and definitely only those with no fear of heights. The highest free fall in Europe at 80 m (262 ft) is just as stomach-churning as it sounds *(right)*. To go even further, take the Free Fall Tilt, which tilts before it falls.

10 Haunted House

With ghosts and ghouls around every corner, the minimum recommended age of entry here is 10 *(left)*. There is a separate admission fee of 40 kr per person.

History

In the early days, Gröna Lund's main attraction was a carousel moved by a horse. Founder Jacob Schultheis's son, Gustav Nilsson, an electrical engineer, laid the foundations of the modern attraction in the 1920s, not only adding many rides, but building the first stage to host performers. Gröna Lund's popularity surged in the 1960s when it became Sweden's major outdoor concert venue. But it remains true to its origins; most of the buildings on the site are structures dating from the 19th century.

No loose items are allowed on any ride. The park has lockers to leave your stuff in. You will need two 10 kr coins to use a locker.

Nordiska Museet

A monument to Sweden's cultural history, Nordiska Museet exhibits everyday life in Sweden from the 16th century to the present. Created by Artur Hazelius, the founder of Skansen (see pp8–9)*, Nordiska Museet is housed in an imposing Renaissance-style building and the entrance features a huge statue of King Gustav Vasa. With over 1.5 million exhibits, visitors are certainly spoilt for choice here – yet, much of the museum reflects simple everyday life in Sweden through the ages.*

Photographs on display in Nordiska Museet

Borrow an audio guide and follow a map to see the best of the museum in an hour. The trip takes you through the galleries high above the main hall, as well as the museum's history and architecture. Guides are available in several languages.

The museum restaurant (same opening hours as the museum) serves hot meals in traditional Swedish style, coffee and freshly baked bread.

- *Map Q4*
- *Djurgårdsvägen 6–16*
- *08 519 546 00*
- *Tram 7; Buses 44, 69 & 76;*
- *Open 10am–5pm year round; Sep–May: 10am–8pm (on Wed)*
- *Adm: 90 kr (adults); under 18s free; Sep–May: free 5–8pm Wed*
- *www.nordiskamuseet.se*

Top 10 Features

1. Power of Fashion – 300 years of Clothing
2. Interiors
3. Traditions
4. Main Hall
5. Sámi life in Sweden
6. Table Settings
7. Strindberg Collection
8. Swedish Folk Art in the 18th and 19th Centuries
9. Dolls' Houses
10. Small Objects 1700–1900

1 Power of Fashion – 300 years of Clothing

Clothing has long been a symbol of a person's identity. Power of Fashion *(above)* looks at clothing from the 1780s, 1860s and 1960s, the times when fashion and looks were influenced by the economy, flow of ideas and technical developments.

2 Interiors

On display are re-created period homes *(right)*, including parts of a drawing room from the 1880s and a Swedish interior from the 1950s.

3 Traditions

Why and when do Swedes eat *semlor*, cream buns with marzipan? What are the origins of the Midsummer pole? Where did traditional Christmas celebrations originate? The answers to these and many other questions can be found in this exhibition, which covers festivals throughout the year.

There is a great playroom with shop interiors, kitchens and farm settings from the old days that kids can play in.

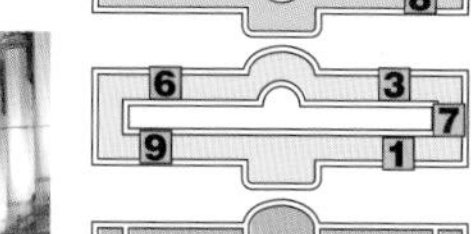

Key

First Floor

Second Floor

Third Floor

4 Main Hall

A fitting entrance to the museum *(right)*, the huge hall's centrepiece is a monumental pink statue of King Gustav Vasa by Carl Milles carved in 1924, in oak – supposedly including wood from a tree planted by the king himself.

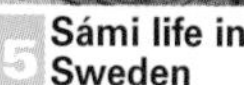

5 Sámi life in Sweden

The Sámi are Europe's northernmost, and the Nordic countries' only, officially indigenous people. This exhibition examines their traditional way of life, struggles and how they have influenced Swedish culture *(above)*.

6 Table Settings

Re-creations of table settings *(left)* from the 16th to 20th centuries highlight customs about food and drink, and how cutlery and drinking vessels have developed.

7 Strindberg Collection

The largest single collection of August Strindberg's paintings is owned by the museum. Sixteen of these are on display, along with photographs taken by Strindberg and several of his original manuscripts.

8 Swedish Folk Art in the 18th and 19th Centuries

Rural folk art blossomed in the 18th and 19th centuries – craftspeople passed on their skills from one generation to the next. Indeed, its heritage lives on today as a big influence on Swedish contemporary design *(right)*.

9 Dolls' Houses

There are fifteen dolls' houses ranging from the 1600s to the present, which reflect the styles and home decor of different periods.

10 Small Objects 1700–1900

Artur Hazelius began getting together items that make up the collection from 1872. As he wandered through rural Sweden, Hazelius acquired a collection of household objects, down to the smallest pin.

August Strindberg

Famous author, theatrical director, painter and photographer, Strindberg (1849–1912) took personal interest in the Nordiska Museet project and contributed ideas. After his death, much of his property was given to the museum.

There are temporary exhibitions on the second and third floors. See the museum's website for what is currently on display.

Historiska Museet

Sweden's National Historical Museum, opened in 1943, focuses on early civilization in Sweden, especially from the initial traces of human societies to the Middle Ages. It is particularly reknowned for its Gold Room. Built in reinforced concrete to ensure security, the Gold Room showcases 52 kg (114 lbs) of gold objects, as well as 250 kg (551 lbs) of silver items, mainly from the Bronze Age to the Middle Ages. Other sections take a fresh approach on presenting historical trends and events up to the present through engaging displays.

Historiska Museet

Audio guides in different languages are available for many of the exhibitions. For children aged six and above, there is a history trail from Viking times through to the Middle Ages.

Café Rosengården (same opening hours as the museum) serves lunch, snacks and drinks. A ticket to the museum is not necessary to use the café.

- *Map Q2*
- *Narvavägen 13–17*
- *08 519 556 00*
- *Tram 7 to Djurgårdsbron; Buses 44, 56, 69 & 76; Underground to Karlaplan*
- *Open 1 Jan–30 Apr & 1 Sep–31 Dec: 11am–5pm Tue–Sun, 1am–8pm Wed; 1 May–31 Aug: 10am–5pm daily, closed at Midsummer; free entry 1–5pm Fri*
- *Adm: 80 kr (adults); 60 kr (students and pensioners); under 18s free*
- *www.historiska.se*

Top 10 Features

1. Gold Room
2. Alunda Elk
3. Bäckaskog Woman
4. History of Sweden
5. Bronze Age Finds
6. Textile Chamber
7. Vikings
8. Maria from Viklau
9. The Skog Tapestry
10. Gothic Hall

1 Gold Room

The priceless artifacts in the Gold Room include Bronze Age jewellery, demonstrating the amazing skills of craftsmen of that era, and a medieval goblet turned reliquary *(above)*.

2 Alunda Elk

This carved stone moose head *(below)* was used as a ceremonial axe; animals such as moose and bear were symbols of the gods in the Stone Age.

3 Bäckaskog Woman

This moving exhibit is the skeleton of a 155-cm (5-ft) tall woman *(below)* who lived in the Stone Age. It tells us that she died at around 45 years of age and that she had borne many children. The skeleton was discovered in the 1930s, buried in a pit.

4 History of Sweden

Discover Swedish history from the 11th century to the present in a series of displays based around events in the lives of famous and lesser known historic persons.

The exhibitions are arranged chronologically on two floors.

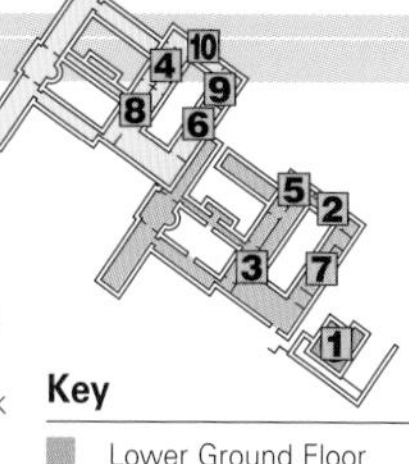

Key

Lower Ground Floor

Ground Floor

First Floor

5 Bronze Age Finds

Priceless artifacts have been uncovered after 3,000 years, often by chance. These include human figures in bronze *(left)* found in Skåne, a gold bowl discovered by an army lieutenant and his daughter out for a walk in 1847, and a gold cup unearthed by a widow in 1859, for which she earned the equivalent of about six months' wages.

6 Textile Chamber

Like altarpieces, textiles *(main image)* were often used to depict stories in churches. The ones that are displayed here are of many styles and patterns.

7 Vikings

Embellished swords of the Vikings are on display here, but shattering many of the myths surrounding the Vikings are objects from everyday life that prove that they mostly led a peaceful existence as traders.

8 Maria from Viklau

Wood has long been a popular material for sculptures in Sweden. This richly gilded figure of the Madonna *(left)* is one of the best early medieval examples, originating from Viklau Church on the island of Gotland, in the 1100s.

9 The Skog Tapestry

This 13th-century tapestry, richly woven with human figures and animals *(left)*, once decorated the walls of a wooden church in Skog in northern Sweden.

10 Gothic Hall

Striking altarpieces and other church items *(above)* from the Middle Ages are on display here. The altarpieces were used to depict Biblical stories to the congregation as most people could not read or write.

Museum Guide

The Prehistory, Viking and temporary exhibitions are on the ground floor, as is the café and museum shop. On the first floor is Medieval Art and the Tapestry Room. The lower ground floor, which houses the Gold Room, can be reached by a staircase from the entrance hall. Disabled access is via a lift to the right of the entrance steps and in the museum. A Braille map is also available.

TOP 10 Hagaparken

A vast green area north of the city, the historic Haga is one of Stockholm's most beloved parks. Created in the late 18th century by King Gustav III, its natural "English" style was a reaction to formal Baroque designs. Some 26,000 trees were planted, interspersed with lawns and winding pathways. Buildings erected between 1786 and 1793 include the Chinese Pavilion, Copper Tents and the Temple of Echo. It is the perfect getaway in any season – in summer, it is popular for picnics, sunbathing or just taking it easy.

Winding pathway shaded by trees in Hagaparken

Download a free English audio guide to the park as an MP3 to your audio player or phone from www.onspotstory.com.

In summer, do as the locals do and bring a picnic hamper. Apart from the lawns, there are many secluded spots and plenty of park benches.

- *Map G2*
- *4 km (2.5 miles) N of Stockholm*
- *08 27 42 52*
- *Bus 52 from Slussen, Sergels Torg and various stops in the city (direction Karolinska Hospital) to Haga Norra or Haga Södra; T-bana to Odenplan, Bus 515 to Haga Södra.*
- *Park: Open year round*
- *Butterfly and Bird House: Open Apr–Sep: 10am–4pm daily; Oct–Mar: 10am–3pm daily, closed Mon.*
- *Adm: 95 kr (adults), 50 kr (4–15s); Family ticket: 260 kr*
- *Haga Parkmuseum: Open 10am–3pm Thu–Sun.*
- *Gustav III's Pavilion: Open Jun–Aug: Tue–Sun by guided tour only*
- *www.kungahuset.se*

Top 10 Features

1. Copper Tents
2. Stora Pelousen
3. Chinese Pagoda
4. Echo Temple
5. Gustav III's Pavilion
6. Butterfly and Bird House
7. Turkish Pavilion
8. Haga Parkmuseum
9. Haga Ruins
10. Cafés

1 Copper Tents

The tents' façades are adorned with painted copper plates *(below)*, giving the illusion of a sultan's encampment. The middle tent houses the park museum.

2 Stora Pelousen

Epitomizing the park's English character, the *Pelouse* – French for lawn – has been a recreational destination for Stockholmers for 200 years. It is a popular sunbathing spot in summer and skiers take over in winter.

3 Chinese Pagoda

The open octagonal building *(main image)* was built in 1787, its tent roof adorned with dragon heads with bells. It was repaired in 1974, and new dragons of toughened plastic replaced the decaying oak ones.

4 Echo Temple

A national monument, this temple *(right)* was built in 1790 as a summer dining room for King Gustav III, who loved to eat al fresco.

The gates at both the northern and southern entrances to the park once stood in Kungsträdgården in the city.

5 Gustav III's Pavilion

Dating from 1787, this pretty little palace *(above)* has light, airy interiors, inspired by the antique Roman villas of Pompeii which had just been discovered.

6 Butterfly and Bird House

Even in the depths of winter the daytime temperature in this tropical rainforest never drops below 25° C (77° F), a thriving habitat for shimmering butterflies, tropical insects, spiders and parrots.

8 Haga Parkmuseum

The original model of the palace that King Gustav III was having built at the time of his assassination in 1792, and which was never completed, is in the museum *(above)*. It also includes information about the people associated with Haga, such as the poet Carl Michael Bellman.

7 Turkish Pavilion

Completed in 1788, the Turkish Pavilion *(above)* was used by King Gustav III to hold meetings with his closest advisors. There are plans to restore the original furnishings, which have been traced among the fittings in the royal palaces.

9 Haga Ruins

Work started on the foundations and cellars of a grand palace in 1786 but ceased when Gustav III was murdered. The palace was never completed.

10 Cafés

The Copper Tents have a coffee shop and picnic room. A small café *(left)* in the park serves home-baked cinnamon buns and snacks.

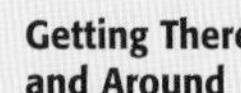

Getting There and Around

Alight from the bus at Haga Södra. Walk past the tennis courts and follow the path by the waters of Brunnsviken, through the woods to the lawns and Copper Tents. On your way back follow the higher path to your right with your back to the Copper Tents. This brings you out through the park's south gates and to the bus stop. Take Bus 59 back to various stops in the city, in the direction of Malmgårdsvägen.

Since 2010, Haga Slott, the main palace, is home to Crown Princess Victoria and closed to the public.

Left **The 16th-century Royal Palace** Right **The Olympics in Stockholm, July 1912**

Top 10 Moments in History

1 1252: Foundation of Stockholm

Stockholm is first mentioned in records in the 13th century. The name probably originates from "stock" (log) and "holm" (islet) – the logs used for building in the Gamla Stan area, particularly the fortress built by the ruler Birger Jarl in 1252. This protected the passage from Lake Mälaren to the Baltic, vital for trade with Germans. The structure burnt down in 1697, and the present-day Royal Palace was built on site.

2 1520: Stockholm Bloodbath

The culmination of a long Danish campaign to take control of Sweden, the Stockholm Bloodbath saw around 80–90 people, mainly clergy and nobility who supported the influential Sture party, being executed one by one at Stortorget, outside the Tre Kronor palace. The event led to severe opposition to Danish rule.

3 1523: King Gustav Vasa

Having avoided the Stockholm Bloodbath, Gustav Vasa led a rebellion against Danish rule; it ended with him being crowned king on 6 June 1523 – Sweden's National Day. Sweden was united under his 37-year rule. This era is seen as the birth of modern Sweden, during which it also became a Protestant country.

King Gustav Vasa

4 1792: Murder of Gustav III

Gustav III was a patron of the arts, literature and theatre; he founded prestigious academies, such as the Swedish Academy and the Royal Opera, and initiated reform programmes. But opposition to his absolute powers and costly foreign policy cost him his life – in 1792, he was shot during a masked ball at Stockholm's Opera House, and died of his wounds 14 days later.

5 1871: Industrialization

The completion of a railway to both the north and the south helped Stockholm begin its rapid, industrial progress. In 1876, Lars Magnus Ericsson founded the Ericsson phone company in the capital, leading the way for Stockholm to establish an extensive phone network.

6 1912: Summer Olympics

The Stockholm Olympic Stadium, built for the 1912 Olympics, is still used as a major sports and concert venue. The games were known as the "Swedish masterpiece" because they were so well organized, and included the first use of electronic timing and public address systems.

7 1936: Rise of the Social Democrats

Dominating Swedish politics from 1936 until the 1980s, the Social

Preceding pages **Colourful houses on an archipelago island**

Democrats established the modern welfare state and shaped the 20th-century development of Stockholm. Poverty was virtually eradicated in the 1930s and 1940s, and almost the entire country was electrified and connected by new roads.

8 1965: Housing Modernization Programme

An apartment construction project from 1965 to1974, known as the Million Programme, succeeded in its aim to build over a million new homes, but got mixed reactions – the main criticism was that many of the blocks were uninspiring.

Olof Palme's grave at Adolf Fredriks Kyrka

9 1986: Olof Palme's Assassination

The killing of popular Prime Minister Olof Palme in central Stockholm on 28 February 1986 shook Sweden to the core. Palme was shot while returning home from the cinema; his murder has never been solved. The reward for finding the killer stands at €5 million.

10 2000: Into the 21st Century

Present-day Sweden is regarded as having a robust economy and seen as a leader in many technological fields as well as design and style. A strong promoter of equal rights, Sweden was ranked third in the 2011 Quality of Life index and joint-first in terms of democracy.

Top 10 Historical Figures

1 Queen Kristina (1626–89)

Kristina "civilized" a warrior nation by bringing philosophers to Stockholm, before moving to Rome and becoming a Catholic.

2 Carl Linneaus (1707–78)

A botanist responsible for the classification of living things, Linneaus travelled extensively to find different species.

3 Alfred Nobel (1833–96)

Holder of 355 different patents, he used his fortune to found the Nobel Prize.

4 August Strindberg (1849–1912)

The father of modern Swedish literature was also a painter and photographer.

5 Tage Erlander (1901–85)

Swedish Prime Minister for an uninterrupted 23 years, Erlander's tenure is a record for parliamentary democracies.

6 Dag Hammarskjöld (1905–61)

Hammarskjöld was the UN Secretary General from 1953 until his death in a plane crash.

7 Greta Garbo (1905–90)

A Hollywood star, Greta Garbo retired at just 43 years of age.

8 Astrid Lindgren (1907–2002)

Internationally acclaimed, her *Pippi Longstocking* series were translated into 64 languages.

9 Ingmar Bergman (1918–2007)

Director and writer of over 60 films, Bergman was described by Woody Allen as "probably the greatest film artist".

10 Olof Palme (1927–86)

Twice Prime Minister and head of the Social Democrats, he majorly shaped domestic and international politics.

The Stockholm Olympic Stadium can be viewed from 8am–9pm Sunday to Friday and 8am–8pm on Saturdays except during events.

Left **Treasury crowns, Royal Palace** Centre **Elk at Skansen** Right **Ceiling painting, Drottningholm**

TOP 10 Museums and Galleries

1 Skansen

Open-air museum, zoo, concert venue, playground and park, Skansen's chief attraction is its collection of buildings from all over Sweden, including a 19th-century town. Traditional crafts, including glassblowing, are practised in the workshops, while the zoo is home to a wide range of Nordic animals, including bear and lynx *(see pp8–9)*.

2 Vasamuseet

The only preserved 17th-century warship in the world, the *Vasa*, despite its impressive appearance, sank shortly after setting sail on its maiden voyage in 1628. Raised 333 years later, in 1961, it proved to be remarkably intact. With three masts projecting from the roof, the *Vasamuseet* is quite a unique attraction *(see pp10–11)*.

Vasamuseet sculpture

3 Drottningholm

One of Stockholm's three World Heritage Sites, Drottningholm comprises a perfectly preserved 17th-century palace and gardens. The official residence of the Swedish Royal family, it is nevertheless open year round; an ideal way to visit in summer is a one-hour boat trip across Lake Mälaren from the city direct to the palace *(see pp18–19)*.

4 Fotografiska Museet

This museum opened in 2010 as a centre for contemporary photography. It presents four big and 20 smaller exhibitions annually. Housed in a former industrial Jugend-style building on Stockholm's waterfront with stunning views, it also has a café-bar serving lunch and snacks *(see p92)*.

Contemporary photographs at Fotografiska Museet

Many museums close over Midsummer's eve and during Christmas holidays.

Fountain sculptures in Millesgården

5 Millesgården

A sculpture park featuring the works of Carl Milles (1875–1955) on the island of Lidingö, Millesgården offers a beautiful view over Stockholm and the harbour. The main building was Milles's studio and home in the later years of his life. The park also has an outdoor restaurant and bistro *(see p98)*.

6 Moderna Museet

This museum has one of the world's finest collections of 20th-century art, including works by Picasso, Henri Matisse and Salvador Dali, and makes ongoing acquisitions of recent contemporary art. It also houses photographic art and photography, spanning from the 1840s to the present day *(see p84)*.

7 Nordiska Museet

Discover Sweden's cultural history in this museum. Exhibitions on trends and traditions, folk art, textiles and fashion, and furnished rooms reveal life in Sweden through the ages. They are housed in a palatial building on Djurgårdsvägen *(see pp24–5)*.

8 Historiska Museet

Sweden's National Historical Museum brings civilization alive from the earliest settlements to the Middle Ages. Highlights include the Vikings, the life of eight different people from prehistory and the Gold Room *(see pp26–7)*.

9 The Royal Palace

The world's biggest palace still used by a head of state, it houses the Royal Apartments, the Hall of State, the Treasury and the Tre Kronor Museum. The magnificent rooms, built from 1697 to 1754, range in style from Rococo to Baroque to Gustavian Neo-Classic *(see pp20–21)*.

10 Nationalmuseet

Paintings and sculptures by great masters such as Rembrandt, Renoir, Rubens, Degas and Gauguin and those by Swedish masters Anders Zorn and Carl Larsson are housed in Sweden's national gallery. The museum is under renovation – some temporary exhibits may be at special locations in the city *(see p85)*.

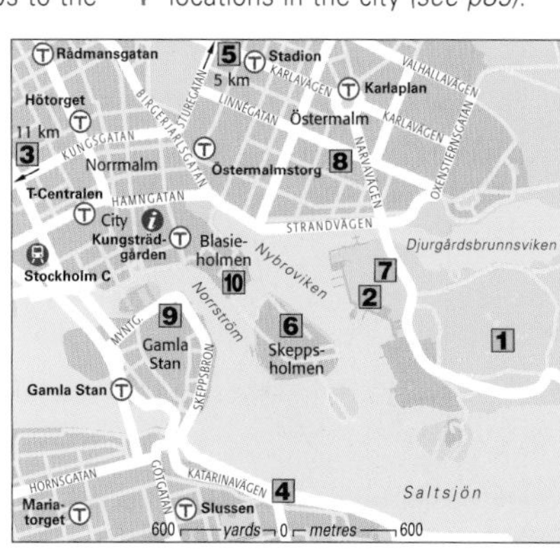

Left **Aquaria Vattenmuseum** Centre **Carousel in Skansen** Right **Leksaksmuseet**

TOP 10 Children's Attractions

Playful exhibits at Junibacken

1 Junibacken

The story-book world of Junibacken in Djurgården opens up like a fantasy adventure. Characters from children's books live around the Storybook Square, with its cobblestones and old-fashioned street lamps. The Story Train transports visitors into the fairy-tale world of Astrid Lindgren and there is a great play area based on well-loved stories. ✆ *Galärvarvsvägen • Map Q4 • 08 587 230 00 • Tram 7; Buses 44 or 69 • Open 10am–5pm Tue–Sun (Jun–Aug: 10am–6pm daily) • Adm • www.junibacken.se*

2 Gröna Lund

There are rides and fairground attractions for children of all ages at this traditional funfair. Do not miss the Fun House, the Mirror Pavilion and the traditional sideshows *(see pp22–3)*.

3 Skansen

Children will love Skansen's animals. The Galejan fairground includes a carousel and sideshows, while the electric cars have delighted youngsters for decades *(see pp8–9)*.

4 Aquaria Vattenmuseum

Find out what it is to be like in a living Amazon rainforest, with giant catfish, stingrays and piranhas, at night or during a tropical thunderstorm. Visitors can get close to sharks and a Baltic exhibit with wild sea trout spawning indoors. The café, with harbour views, is a good place to relax. ✆ *Falkenbergsgatan 2 • Map Q5 • 08 660 90 89 • Tram 7; Buses 44 or 69 • Open 10am–4:30pm Tue–Sun • Adm • www.aquaria.se*

Performer in Gröna Lund

5 Naturhistoriska Riksmuseet

Explore the history of life and the Earth, or go on an expedition to the North and South Poles. Visitors can study the electric current in the brain, test their reliability as eyewitnesses or challenge their senses in the Dark Room at 39 interactive stations. There are digital shows at Cosmonova's IMAX cinema *(see p98)*.

6 Leksaksmuseet

The museum has functioning model railways and Disney figures from the 1930s. There are thousands of toys from over the centuries – cuddly teddy bears, dolls and dolls' houses from as far back as the 16th century, as well as toy boats, cars, aeroplanes and motorbikes. *Tegelviksgatan 22 • Map F6 • 08 641 61 00 • Bus 2 or 66 • Open 10am–5pm Mon–Fri, 11am–4pm Sat & Sun • Adm • www.leksaksmuseet.se*

Puppets in Musik and Teatermuseet

7 Swimming pools

Eriksdalsbadet, Stockholm's main swimming pool, has adventure pools for children and an outdoor pool in summer. The main adventure pool is comfortably warm and 1.4 m (4 ft) deep with two slopes. The outdoor pool is open from late May to late August. *Hammarby slussväg 20 • 08 508 402 58 • Adm*

8 Fjärderholmarna

This island, a short boat trip from Stockholm, is an ideal children's day out. Activities include pottery and textile printing, climbing a pirate ship and petting rabbits. There are play and picnic areas and the path around the island's perimeter is stroller friendly *(see p12)*.

9 Musik and Teatermuseet

Children and adults can play instruments, while displays showcase aspects of the world of music. A varied programme of regular activities includes musical games for children, puppet workshops and interactive concerts. *Sibyllegatan 2 • Map N2 • 08 519 554 90 • Open noon–5pm Tue–Sun • Adm • www.musikmuseet.se*

10 Ice-skating rinks

Kungsträdgården *(see p62)* in the city centre, Medborgarplatsen *(see p91)* on Södermalm, Vasaparken *(see p70)* in Vasastan all have outdoor skating rinks in winter. Several ice-hockey rinks are also open to the public. Visit the tourist office for an up-to-date list.

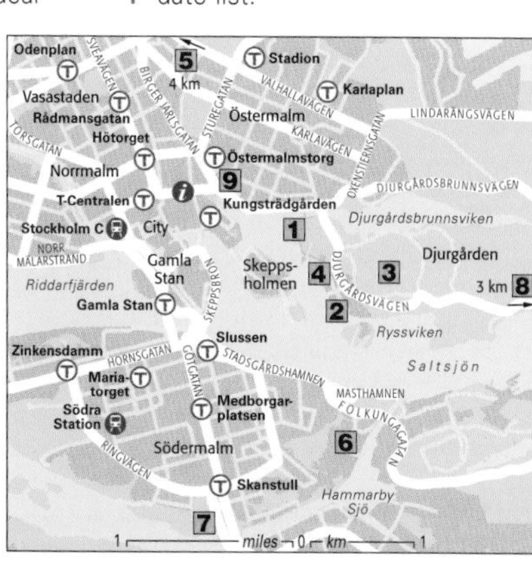

There are good playgrounds in Humlegarden (see p75) and Vasaparken (see p70).

Left **Band performing at Popaganda** Right **Children at the Stockholm Culture Festival**

TOP 10 Festivals and Events

1 Stockholm International Film Festival

Inaugurated in 1990, this two-week long event in mid-November hosts film screenings all around the city, with an emphasis on new and upcoming directors. Other highlights through the year include a mini-outdoor festival in August. *www.stockholmfilmfestival.se*

2 Stockholm Marathon

Attracting 21,000 runners worldwide, this marathon takes place on the last Saturday in May or the first in June, with the finish in the classic Olympic Stadium. Book both the race and accommodation in advance. *www.stockholmmarathon.se*

3 Popaganda

Stockholm's biggest pop festival is held at Eriksdalsbadet's outdoor baths *(see p37)* over two days at the end of August and focuses on indie pop with a mix of well-established and newer artists. *www.popaganda.se*

4 Stockholm International Horse Show

Equestrian sport is the second most popular sport in Sweden. The Stockholm International Horse Show hosts international competitions as well as Icelandic horse displays at Globen *(see p98)* over three days at the end of November or beginning of December. *www.stockholmhorseshow.com*

5 Stockholm Pride

Pride Parade, with over 50,000 participants and 500,000 spectators, is the highlight of this week-long gay pride festival held at the end of July or beginning of August. The parade is a celebration of human rights and openness; other events include Pride Park, featuring concerts and stalls. *www.stockholmpride.org*

6 Nobel Day

On 10 December, the anniversary of Alfred Nobel's death, the Nobel Prize is awarded in Stockholm in the areas of Physics, Chemistry, Medicine, Literature and Economics. After the award ceremony, a widely telecast banquet with 1,300 guests is held in Stockholm City Hall.

7 DN Galan

The largest annual sporting event in Sweden, DN Galan is an international track and field event in mid-August. Held at the 1912 Olympic Stadium, it is part of the International Association of

Stockholm International Horse Show

Dates for many festivals and events vary from year to year – check the events' websites for the latest information.

Athletes at the DN Galan event

Athletics Federations' Diamond League – the world's foremost one-day athletic meeting circuit. *www.diamondleague-stockholm.com*

8 **Midnattsloppet**
The "Midnight race" is run over 10 km (6 miles) by 24,000 runners from around 9:30pm in the Södermalm district of Stockholm in mid-August; people run well into the night. There are 16 starting groups ensuring that all ability levels are catered for, from the serious to a masquerade in outrageous fancy dress and the party goes on till late in the night. *www.midnattsloppet.com*

9 **Stockholm Culture Festival**
Held in the month of August, this festival hosts performances and acts such as dance, music and mime on streets, squares and stages throughout the centre. There is a mini children's festival where kids can play, dance, sing and listen to stories. *www.kulturfestivalen.stockholm.se*

10 **Stockholm Fashion Week**
The Swedish Fashion Council stages fashion events each year – January/February and August see the major fashion weeks. Other related activities organized during the season include exhibitions, trade fairs and press events.
www.stockholmfashionweek.com

Top 10 National Holidays and Celebrations

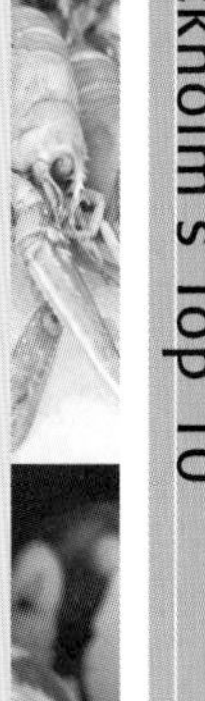

1 **New Year's Eve, 31 December**
Locals spill out onto the streets a few minutes before midnight to enjoy fireworks displays.

2 **Easter**
Traditions include egg painting and consumption of sweets hidden in paper eggs.

3 **Walpurgis night, 30 April**
A traditional northern European spring festival, Valborg is marked with bonfires and parties.

4 **1 May**
A national holiday marked by the Social Democratic party and labour groups marching in the city centre.

5 **Ascension Day, June**
Since this falls on a Thursday, many workers take a *klämdag* or a day off on Friday for a long weekend.

6 **National Day, 6 June**
A public holiday since 2005, this day marks the date of King Gustav Vasa's ascension to the throne.

7 **Midsummer, June**
One of the year's biggest holidays. Skansen is a great place to join in the summer solstice celebrations.

8 **Crayfish season, August**
Parties involve shelling the fish by hand and having schnapps.

9 **Lucia, 13 December**
White robed girls sing traditional Christmas songs in candlelit processions at schools, churches and work-places; saffron buns are eaten.

10 **Christmas, 24–26 December**
Families gather on Christmas Eve to celebrate with a traditional *julbord*, the Christmas equivalent of a *smörgåsbord*.

Stockholm public transport operates on all holidays including Christmas and usually follows the Sunday timetable.

Left **Display in a SoFo shop** Centre **Food counter at Östermalms Saluhall** Right **Urban Outfitters**

Top 10 Places to Shop

1 NK

Stockholm's most luxurious department store, Nordiska Kompaniet (NK) was established in 1902. Many Swedish and international fashion labels have their stores here. There are items for the home, souvenirs and a food store. *Hamngatan 18–20 • Map M3 • 08 762 80 00 • Open 10am–8pm Mon–Fri, 10am–6pm Sat, 11am–5pm Sun*

2 PUB

This is Stockholm's oldest department store – Greta Garbo used to work in a hat shop here. PUB has recently rebranded itself as a premier retailer for fashion and design. *Hötorget • Map L2 • 08 789 19 30 • Open 10am–7pm Mon–Fri, 10am–6pm Sat, 11am–5pm Sun*

3 Gallerian

Central Stockholm's largest shopping mall houses over 80 fashion labels, cafés and restaurants. It is also home to the budget hardware store Clas Ohlson. *Hamngatan 37 • Map M3 • 08 533 373 00 • Open 10am–8pm Mon–Fri, 10am–6pm Sat, 11am–6pm Sun*

4 SoFo

The name, meaning "South of Folkungagatan", is a word play on the Soho districts of London and New York. This quarter has design and fashion shops, as well as restaurants and bars. The last Thursday of every month is SoFo Night, when retailers are open till 9pm. *Map E5 • Open 11am–6pm Mon–Fri, 11am–5pm Sat, noon–4pm Sun*

5 Östermalms Saluhall

Named "The world's 7th-best food hall" by *Bon Appétit* magazine, this building retains many of the original features from when it opened in 1888. There are 17 specialist stalls as well as full à la carte dining. *Östermalmstorg • Map N2 • Open 9:30am–8pm Mon–Thu, 9:30am–6:30pm Fri, 9:30am–4pm Sat*

6 H&M

H&M has become a worldwide name for affordable trendy clothing for all ages. There are shops all over Stockholm and Sweden, but the Hamngatan store is where the latest styles arrive first. *Hamngatan 22 • Map M3 • 08 524 635 30 • Open 10am–8pm Mon–Fri, 10am–6pm Sat, 11am–6pm Sun*

7 Åhléns City

The flagship store of Sweden's biggest chain of department stores (18 shops in Stockholm and its suburbs alone) includes a grocery store. *Klarabergsgatan 50 • Map L3 • 08 402 80 00 • Open 10am–7pm Mon–Fri, 10am–6pm Sat, 11am–5pm Sun*

Shoppers in Åhléns City

Most shops open at 10am; supermarkets and food stores open earlier.

Sturegallerian's contemporary decor

8 **Sturegallerian**
This exclusive shopping gallery features 60 retailers selling Swedish and international designs, fashion, jewellery and household items. It is also home to Hedengrens, one of the city's best bookstores. *Stureplan 4 • Map M2 • 08 453 52 00 • Open 10am–7pm Mon–Fri, 10am–5pm Sat, noon–5pm Sun*

9 **Urban Outfitters**
This funky store sells an esoteric blend of ironic and trendy clothing, household goods, books, music and novelty items. Housed in a former cinema, the branch in Stockholm pulls off its image with aplomb. *Biblioteksgatan 5 • Map M2 • 08 545 065 90 • Open 10am–7pm Mon–Fri, 10am–6pm Sat, noon–5pm last Sun of every month*

10 **Götgatan**
From the Götgatan exit of Slussen underground to Skrapan, a former tax office high-rise now converted into a galleria on the lower floors, Götgatan is a street lined with all types of shops, from old-style lamps sellers to some of Sweden's top fashion and design brands. The pace and atmosphere is more relaxed than in the city and there is no shortage of refreshment stops. *Map D6*

Top 10 Things to Buy

1 **Aquavit**
A spirit flavoured with spices and herbs; buy a set of miniature bottles to sample the different varieties.

2 **Children's Toys**
Sweden takes toy design seriously, and colourful, durable wooden toys are a great choice.

3 **Clothing**
Emulate Stockholmers at budget H&M and Weekday, or splash out on top brands.

4 **Dala Horse**
A classic Swedish symbol, delightful wooden Dala horses come in various sizes.

5 **Designer Objects**
All manner of cool items for the home tempt and inspire in Stockholm's abundant design stores.

6 **Gingerbread Biscuits**
Delicious *pepparkakor* biscuits can be bought at all supermarkets or gift packed at department stores.

7 **Lingonberry and Cloudberry Jams**
Lingonberry jam is the traditional accompaniment to meatballs while the sweet cloudberry makes a tasty topping on waffles.

8 **Salt Liquorice**
Definitely an acquired taste but amusing to take home and offer friends. They may just love it!

9 **Swedish Glass**
Sweden is renowned for beautiful glass and crystal ware; watch it being blown at Skansen.

10 **Swedish Pop Music**
From ABBA to Robyn and Lykke Li, Sweden has long been a great exporter of music, so drop by a record store for the next big thing in music.

Some stores, particularly outside the city centre, maintain the tradition of closing at 1pm or 3pm on Saturdays.

Left **Interior of the F12** Centre **The well-stocked Nytroget Urban Deli** Right **Grill's bar counter**

TOP 10 Restaurants

1 Sturehof

Bustling and cool, this classy seafood restaurant with an excellent reputation focuses on Swedish-French home cooking – the wide-ranging menu follows the seasons, complemented by a huge wine list. Pricey, yet reasonable by Stockholm standards for exclusive cuisine *(see p79)*.

2 F12

Star chef Danyel Couet has run F12 since 1994. His philosophy is creative composition of ingredients – innovative, international cooking with rare flavour combinations. Several waiters and waitresses are qualified sommeliers, and the wine list as well as the food changes with the seasons *(see p67)*.

3 Grill

As the name implies, this place is all about grilled food, with the emphasis on meat, but with some fish dishes as well. The atmosphere is playful and relaxed with DJs and live music – also a great place to drop by for a drink. The Happy Sundays buffet is a good-value option at the weekend *(see p73)*.

4 Cloud Nine Food and Cocktails

Be transported to the old world of France in its colonial heyday. The main dining room is adorned with old French travel posters and is ideal for a cosy winter evening. By contrast, the outdoor plaza comes alive in summer – despite being in the city, the courtyard is peaceful with tables in the sun or shade and friendly staff in attendance *(see p67)*.

5 Pelikan

One of the few surviving traditional Swedish beer hall-restaurants, Pelikan is said to date from the 1660s – its retro wood-panelling and down-to-earth Swedish fare is popular with people of all types and ages, whether for a meal or just a beer in the bar *(see p95)*.

6 Nytorget Urban Deli

In keeping with the trendy SoFo area, Urban Deli has a New York-style atmosphere: it is a restaurant, bar, deli and store all rolled into one. The atmosphere is unpretentious; families with children will feel at home *(see p95)*.

7 Mathias Dahlgren

A visit to this restaurant in the Grand Hotel is a gastronomic event. The theme, however, is not ostentatious; simplicity combines with great attention to

Seating outside Cloud Nine Food and Cocktails

While several restaurants advertise late opening hours, last orders for food may be earlier.

detail. The food is Swedish with global influences on a daily changing menu. Prices match an exclusive dining experience *(see p112)*.

8 **Nostrano**

Intimate neighbourhood restaurants are not so easy to find in Stockholm, but Nostrano ticks all the right boxes. Tucked away on a little side street in Södermalm, this little Italian restaurant has replicated the feel of the local's choice in an Italian town. Pre-booking is strongly advised *(see p95)*.

Traditional Swedish fare, Ulla Winbladh

9 **Ulla Winbladh**

Step back in time at this traditional restaurant in a peaceful setting on Djurgården. The menu serves classic Swedish food: reindeer, fried beef, fish stew or boiled cod. An outdoor terrace and lounge is open during the summer. A popular spot; book ahead *(see p79)*.

10 **Gondolen**

A unique location with possibly the best restaurant view in Stockholm, Gondolen is suspended 33 m (108 ft) above Slussen, looking out over the water. Prices are upmarket, though the restaurant's "back pocket" has cheaper deals without the view, which you can still enjoy at a pre- or post-meal drink in the main bar *(see p95)*.

Top 10 Swedish Foods and Drinks

1 **Swedish meatballs**

The classic Swedish *köttbullar* are made with ground beef and served with mashed potato and lingonberry jam.

2 **Cinnamon buns**

Kanelbulle, the perfect accompaniment to coffee or tea, is found in almost every café.

3 **Smörgåsbord**

A spread of different hot and cold dishes that varies according to the event or season.

4 **Pytt i panna**

A classic Swedish "hash" based around diced, fried potatoes with meat, fish or even vegetarian meat substitute.

5 **Semla**

A bun with almond paste and whipped cream, traditionally eaten around Shrove Tuesday.

6 **Västerbotten cheese**

The king of Swedish cheeses is hard, salty, cow's milk cheese. Also try mature Prästost of Grevé.

7 **Surströmming**

Fermented, tinned, raw herring, eaten in August. Very pungent, and the tin must only be opened outdoors.

8 **Cloudberries**

A delicacy that flourishes only in cold climates. Enjoy cloudberry jam with ice cream or waffles.

9 **Must**

Non-alcoholic drink with spices, hops and malt, giving it a sweet beery taste. Mostly drunk at Christmas and Easter.

10 **Swedish beers**

Swedish beer culture is on the up; try a brew from one of Sweden's flourishing microbreweries.

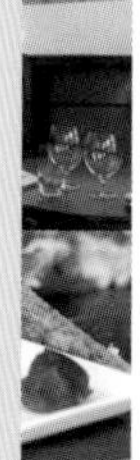

Many restaurants offer good-value Sunday menus and daily lunch offers.

PLUS
PLUS
meny
2:-

Left **Stools at Vurma** Right **Mouthwatering goodies on display in Vete-Katten**

Cafés

1 Saturnus

Everything is big at Saturnus – steaming bowls of café latte and, legend has it, the biggest, and among the best, cinnamon buns in town. It also has a wide range of hot food with good lunches and breakfasts – big as well as small. The theme is colourful and French with a New York twist *(see p78)*.

2 Kaffe

Modern yet simple traditions prevail at Kaffe. There is great coffee at reasonable prices, enjoyed by lots of 30-something freelancers whiling away the afternoon on their laptops or mums and dads on parental leave catching up. Does not accept credit cards. *Sankt Paulsgatan 17 • Map D5 • Open 8am–6pm Mon–Fri, 10am–6pm Sat–Sun*

Outside seating at Kaffe

Cinnamon buns, pastries and cakes, Saturnus

3 Sosta

Consistently rated by coffee connoisseurs as one of the best espresso bars in the city, Sosta has two branches – one located at Jakobsbergsgatan 5 and the other at Sveavägen 84. Most unusually for Sweden, the baristi in this espresso bar are decked out in uniform of striped ties and blue shirts and the quality of coffee is to match. What's more, there is a fine pastry selection *(see p66)*.

4 Vete-Katten

The "wheat cat" was opened in 1928 and still looks like an old-fashioned Swedish café. It offers traditional local cakes with lots of marzipan, and different types of buns. While its front entrance is on the busy central street of Kungsgatan, it also has a quiet courtyard at the back that is open in the summer *(see p66)*.

Preceding pages **Dining room at Berns**

5 Konditori Ritorno

Ritorno is a reminder of 1960s Stockholm cafés with its custom-made neon signs and dark interiors. Its lounge is little altered since it opened in 1959: dark wood, gloomy yet welcoming. Food and drink is simple with the Swedish tradition of helping yourself to coffee and as many refills as you want. There is also an open-air area on the pavement in summer *(see p72)*.

6 Vurma

With a dazzling array of sandwiches that have the oddest names, such as "Freak" and "Aunt", there really is something for everyone, including vegetarians and vegans, at Vurma. It is bohemian, colourful and a bit shabby, but evidently popular, and there are now branches at Birger Jarlsgatan 36, Polhemsgatan 15, Bergsunds Strand 31 and Gastrikgatan 2 *(see p72)*.

7 Petite France

Award-winning bakery and café in the best French tradition, hidden on a side street not far from the waterfront of Lake Mälaren, Petite France serves great croissants and brioches. Breakfast is a treat here and they also do lunches *(see p72)*.

8 Rosendals Trädgård

A summer paradise, Trädgård showcases organic cultivation to the public. Naturally all food is organically grown and there is also a bakery and a shop. It is idyllic to sit at an outdoor table during spring and summer. However, although pricey, it is exceptionally popular at weekends – choose a weekday to avoid the crowds. Check their website for latest opening times *(see p78)*.

9 Valhallabagariet

At the forefront of Stockholm's sourdough bread craze – and with good reason – Valhallabagariet has excellent stone-baked breads, which the locals arrive early to buy. You can enjoy coffee and a raspberry brioche indoors or outdoors *(see p78)*.

10 Mellqvist Kaffebar

Artists, newspaper cartoonists, students and young parents frequent this Södermalm institution from dawn until dusk – Kaffebar seems always busy whatever the day or time, but it has recently expanded, making it easier to find a seat. In summer, and winter, thanks to outdoor heating, people can sit outside. It serves great coffee and terrific cardamom buns *(see p94)*.

Cardamom buns in Mellqvist Kaffebar

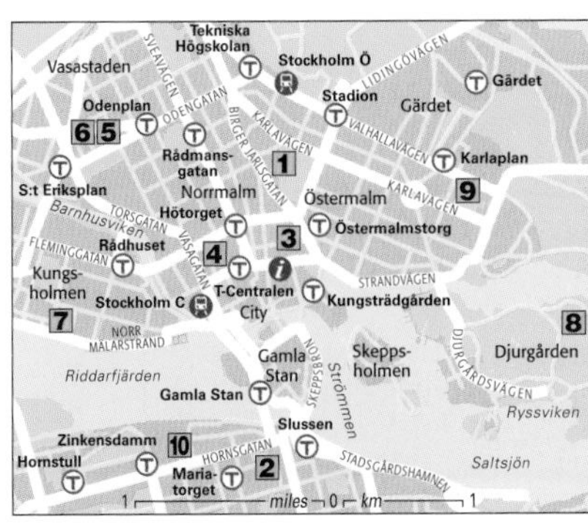

Left **Exterior of Café Tranan** Right **Interior of Cadier Bar**

Top 10 Pubs and Bars

1 Riche

Opened in 1896 with an interior and character inspired by the famous Café Riche in Paris, Riche retains an air of elegance and its menu is based around French-Swedish fusion. The media, fashion and art crowd gather here to listen to unconventional DJ sets from Tuesdays to Saturdays. It is also open for breakfast *(see p78)*.

2 Monks Café and Brewery

A paradise for beer aficionados, not only does Monks Café brew its own ales, but serves over 500 kinds of beer from 50 countries. There is almost always a themed beer festival such as the Porter Festival or the British Beer Festival going on; it also hosts tastings. Monks Café serves classic dishes and the food is fairly priced but the beer is expensive even by Stockholm standards *(see p66)*.

3 Café Tranan

This cosy basement bar, dating back to 1929, is second home to Vasastan's music crowd and attracts a good selection of DJs. Friendly and unpretentious, it is crowded on weekends but is also an excellent choice as a place with a bit of life on a weekday evening. The fried herring with mashed potatoes has been a constant on the menu since it opened *(see p72)*.

4 Kvarnen

One of the few surviving old-style beer halls, Kvarnen serves beer and traditional Swedish food, including good lunches, in a retro atmosphere. Its adjoining nightclub-bar is by contrast decorated with bright blue and white tiles and chrome. Kvarnen is also the pub of Hammarby Football Club and gets crowded and very noisy before home matches *(see p94)*.

Kvarnen's traditional beer hall

5 Kåken

A super trendy annexe to Restaurant 1900, the dark wood and velvet in Kåken is said to be inspired by the American movies of the 1940s – with an American-style grill menu to match. It is popular right from opening time as it attracts the after-work media crowd, and DJs spin sounds that no one else has heard yet *(see p66)*.

Bartender at Kåken

6 Marie Laveau

Lively and large, this hip New York-style bar has an adjoining Cajun restaurant and a nightclub in the basement. Its laid-back evening attitude transforms when DJs take over from around 9pm except during summer. It offers a big brunch menu on Sundays *(see p94)*.

7 Södra Bar

Boasting fine views across Stockholm, Södra Bar is upstairs from Södra Teatern, a great venue for music, theatre and debate. The bar presents an eclectic range of live acts against the background of original decor from a century ago. It can get very crowded but feels more spacious in summer when its veranda is open. *Mosebacke Torg 1–3 • Map D5 • 08 531 993 79 • Open 5pm–1am Tue–Sat*

8 Cadier Bar, Grand Hotel

Elegant yet relaxed, the Cadier Bar reflects the opulence of the Grand Hotel, but everyone is welcome to drop by for a drink and to enjoy the view across the water to the Royal Palace. Some guests may spend 250,000 kr on a 1914 vintage champagne, but it also has affordable quality wines and its cocktails are renowned. *Södra Blasieholmshamnen 8 • Map N4 • 08 679 35 00 • Open 7am–2am Mon–Fri, 8am–2am Sat, 8am–1am Sun*

9 Morfar Ginko and Pappa Ray Ray

These are two venues in one – next to each other and under the same ownership. The mood is laid-back with excellent food and a popular cava bar serving tapas from the counter, which is very unusual for Stockholm. There is a secret courtyard at the back that is open during the summer *(see p94)*.

10 Söders Hjärta

One of the city's most friendly bars, Söders Hjärta's pinball machines indicate its down-to-earth approach. The reasonably priced drinks attract all manner of clientele who feel equally comfortable in groups or popping in on their own to sit at the bar *(see p94)*.

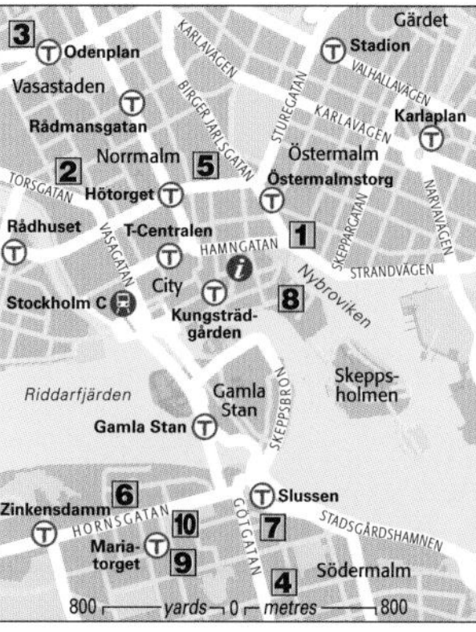

Left **Sturecompagniet's plush sitting area** Right **Drinks at Strand**

Clubs and Nightspots

1 Trädgården

Somehow ramshackle yet stylish, this outdoor summer-only club with live bands, dance floor, bars and food outlets is a huge favourite among the hipster and alternative crowd. It opens in the late afternoon for food and drink, but only gets really busy around midnight. *Hammarby Slussväg 2 • 08 644 20 23 • www.tradgarden.com*

2 Debaser

Named after the Pixies song of the same name, Debaser's roots are in indie rock, but its gigs and clubs cover all ranges of the alternative spectrum. The original club, at Slussen, has the edgier dive bar feel, while Debaser Medis is more for the hip and happening crowd. Both clubs offer free admission before 10pm on Fridays and Saturdays, even when hosting gigs. Debaser Slussen's outdoor bar and restaurant is open earlier in summer. *Map D5 • Debaser Slussen: Karl Johans Torg 1 • 08 30 56 20 • Debaser Medis: Medborgarplatsen 8 • 08 694 79 00 • www.debaser.se*

Façade of the Spy Bar nightclub

3 Café Opera

With royalty and megastars on its guest list, Café Opera is the place to be seen in. Housed in an elegant 19th-century building, its dance-oriented club nights attract clients of all ages. *Karl XII's Torg • Map D3 • 08 676 58 07 • Open 10pm–3am Wed–Sun • Adm • www.cafeopera.se*

4 Sturecompagniet

This nightclub has four halls on two levels around a beautiful atrium. Each has its own musical style. It attracts people from their mid-20s to mid-30s. Come early on weekends as it can be hard to get in after 1am. *Sturegatan 4 • Map D2 • 073 448 66 30 • Open 10pm–3am Thu–Sat*

5 Spy Bar

A legendary survivor in the heart of Stureplan, Spy Bar attracts media folk and serious clubbers and plays everything from funk, alternative disco to rock and pop. It attracts big crowds at weekends. *Birger Jarlsgatan 20 • Map M1 • 08 545 076 55 • Open 10pm–5am Wed–Sat • www.thespybar.se*

6 Golden Hits

This unpretentious club with a nostalgic feel plays pop hits, karaoke and shows. The emphasis is on fun, with a lower age limit of 25, it is popular with singles. *Kungsgatan 29 • Map C2 • 08 505 560 00 • Open early evening–2am Wed & Thu, early evening–3am Fri & Sat • www.goldenhits.se*

Interior of Golden Hits

7 Solidaritet

Electronic dance is the theme of this club with top Swedish and international DJs playing to an open-minded, relaxed crowd. With its warm colours, it has a summery feel whatever the weather. To be on their guest list you can email them through the website. *Lästmakargatan 3 • Map M2 • 08 678 10 50 • www.sldrtt.se*

8 Fasching

Founded in 1977, Fasching is a classic jazz, soul, reggae and latin club that attracts an audience of all ages. It also has a restaurant, open two hours before concert and club nights. *Kungsgatan 63 • Map C3 • 08 534 829 60 • Open 6pm–1am Mon–Wed, 6pm–3am Thu, 6pm–4am Fri–Sat, 5pm–1am Sun • www.fasching.se*

9 Berns

Founded in 1863, Berns is a curious mix of 19th-century splendour and modern style. It has a huge dining room and bars, including an outdoor terrace in summer. Club nights have international DJs and it also hosts top artists for concerts. *Berzelii Park • Map N3 • 08 566 322 00 • Club: open 10pm–early morning Wed–Sat • www.berns.se*

10 Strand

The young crowd heads to Strand for its eclectic live performances and DJs. Club nights are on Fridays and Saturdays, sometimes with a band earlier in the evening. Midweek is more for live music. *Hornstull Strand 4 • Map A5 • 08 658 63 50 • Open 6pm–2am Wed & Thu, 6pm–3am Fri & Sat • www.hornstullstrand.se*

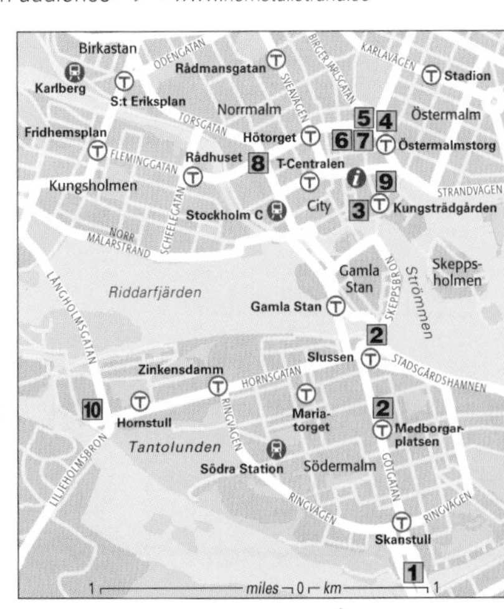

Left **Tantolunden** Right **Paved walking path through Humlegården**

TOP 10 Parks and Gardens

1 Hagaparken

A natural "English" landscaped park, Hagaparken is loved for its tree-lined avenues, beautiful lawns and royal buildings. A highlight is the tropical butterfly house, also home to exotic birds. Enjoy lunch or a snack inside the blue Copper Tents *(see pp28–9)*.

2 Bergianska Trädgården

Near the pretty Brunnsviken waterside walk, the Bergianska botanic garden dates back to the 18th century but shifted to its current location in 1885. Tropical plants bloom in the Orangery and Edvard Anderson Conservatory, which are used for research by Stockholm University. The orangery has a café. *Frescati, 5 km (3 miles) N of central Stockholm • Bus 40 or 540; Universitetet underground • Conservatory and Orangery: open 11am–5pm daily; 11am–4pm in winter • Edvard Anderson Conservatory: adm • www.bergianska.se*

3 Tantolunden

This park in Södermalm is a popular summer hangout for picnics and includes cafés and mini-golf. Do not miss the chance to take a stroll up the hill to enjoy the quaint allotment gardens and good views. There is a pleasant waterside walk from Tanto to Hornstull *(see p91)*.

4 Djurgården

No trip to Stockholm is complete without visiting Djurgården. Not only is it home to several of the city's major museums and attractions – notably Skansen *(see pp8–9)* – but this royal park is an extensive area of greenery with excellent walks and views across the water. Do not miss Rosendals Trädgård, a garden practising biodynamic agriculture, with an excellent café *(see p47)*. *Map G4 • Tram 7 to Djurgården; get off at Skansen or the terminus at Waldermarsudde*

Bergianska Trädgården

Sofia Kyrka in Vitabergsparken

5 Vitabergsparken

This hilly park – the White Mountains Park – in Södermalm includes an open-air theatre hosting free summer concerts and dance performances of all kinds. At its highest point is Sofia Kyrka, a church built in 1911. Wooden workmen's cottages line the park, a reminder that this trendy area was once Stockholm's poorest. There is also one of the city's oldest allotment gardens, dating from 1906. ⊗ *Map E6*

6 Kungsträdgården

A lively leafy square very close to the main shopping areas, Kungsträdgården, or "King's Garden", has numerous cafés and restaurants along its perimeter. Enjoy the "tunnel" of cherry blossom in spring, concerts in summer and ice-skating and a Christmas market in winter *(see p62)*.

7 Humlegården

Oak trees and lawns characterize this central green oasis dating back to the 16th century, but open to the public since 1869. It includes a large playground and skateboard ramp and is also home to the National Library of Sweden. Debaser nightclub *(see p50)* has a summer bar and restaurant here open from late April to the end of August *(see p75)*.

8 Stora Skuggan

Stora Skuggan is a popular recreational venue with open areas. In its centre is a youth-run city farm with animals to meet and greet, and a café in an 18th-century building nearby. ⊗ *Bus 40 to Stora Skuggan*

9 Skinnarviksparken

Head to this park to picnic with the locals. Featuring a wonderful view across Riddarfjärden and of the city, it is ideal for long summer evenings. The park features Arne Jones's stainless steel sculpture, *Progression*. There is a small summer café-kiosk and a playground. ⊗ *Map B5*

10 Vasaparken

Lying between the squares of St Eriksplan and Odenplan, Vasaparken offers many recreational activities. From November to March there is a mechanically frozen ice rink, keeping the ice good whatever the weather *(see p70)*.

Left **Joggers** Centre **Swimmers at an outdoor pool** Right **A game of *boule* in a park**

Top 10 Sporting Activities

1 Tennis

There is no shortage of tennis courts in Stockholm. To play in luxury – at a price – head for the Kungliga Tennishallen, venue for the international Stockholm Open tournament. Tennisstadion, near the Olympic Stadium, also has excellent facilities, but there are many clubs with indoor and outdoor courts for hire, including Hellas Tennisklubb. *Kungliga Tennishallen: 08 459 15 00 • Tennisstadion: 08 54 52 52 54 • Hellas Tennisklubb: 08 640 78 64*

2 Golf

There are about 80 courses around Stockholm to choose from, but green fees can be exorbitant. An excellent choice is Årsta Golf, easily reachable from the centre, with a 9-hole mini-course (120 kr) and a driving range. *www.arstagolf.se*

3 Skating

Kungsträdgården *(see p62)* offers classic ice-skating experience in the city (late November to early March). Rent skates, or bring your own and skate for free; no bookings. *www.kungstradgarden.se*

4 Camping and Hiking

The Right of Public Access makes both camping and hiking in Stockholm and its surroundings a pleasure. Hiking trails offer great views amidst historic settings. For a campsite with toilets and fresh water close to the centre, go to Bredäng Camping, located near the Bredäng underground. *Hiking: www.sormlandsleden.se • www.upplandsstiftelsen.se • www.roslagen.se • Camping: www.bredangcamping.se*

5 Swimming

Stockholm city runs several well-kept municipal indoor pools; Eriksdalsbadet *(see p37)* is the biggest. Do not miss the indoor Art Nouveau Centralbadet *(see p61)*. In summer, take a dip by several beaches; the popular Långholmen *(see p93)* can get crowded if the weather is good.

Ice-skating rink at Kungsträdgården

6 Jogging

The Swedish Heart and Lung Association has around 20 marked routes ideal for jogging and running. Download a map from the website – select the page *Hitta en stig nära dig*, and select "Stockholm" from the drop-down menu. *www.halsansstig.se*

You can buy tickets for many sports events at www.ticnet.se.

7 Brännboll

A popular recreational game similar to rounders, *brännboll* is very easy to play as the batsman simply throws the ball up and strikes it, either with a baseball-type bat or a flat paddle. *Brännboll* sets can be bought in all sports shops. Informal games are played in parks during summer.

Cyclists on a sunny morning

8 Cycling

Bicycle lanes run throughout the city for safe, easy cycling. You can hire modern bicycles, with automatic lights and a basket, from Stockholm City Bikes and pick up and leave them at 70 automated sites *(see p106)*. *www.citybikes.se*

9 Fitness Clubs

There are several sports associations and fitness centres in Stockholm. Friskis & Svettis, SATS Sports Club and Saga in Mariatorget *(see p92)* are some of them. *www.web.friskissvettis.se • www.sats.se • www.sagamotion.nu*

10 Boule

Boule is a very popular sport in Stockholm. At the 10-day Maria Boule festival in early July, you can borrow *boule* for a fee and find a spot to play in Mariatorget; there is also a bar, food and entertainment. Vasaparken has free *boule* courts (*see p70)*. *www.hem.passagen.se/mariaboule*

Top 10 Sports Events

1 Handball
A popular winter sport. The men's and women's national sides often play at Globen.

2 Ice Hockey
One of Sweden's most popular sports. Djurgården and AIK are the city's major teams.

3 Trotting
Bet on harness racing, one of the biggest gambling activities, at Solvalla Stadium.

4 International football
Sweden's national side plays at Råsunda Stadium, Solna; the women's team is as popular as the men's. Tickets are reasonable.

5 DN Galan
Major annual international track and field competition in the Olympic Stadium.

6 Stockholm Open Tennis
ATP tour indoor tournament, attracting some of the world's top players, is held in late October/early November.

7 Stockholm Cup, horse-racing
The Group 3 Stockholm Cup is the season's highlight at the tidy American-style Täby racecourse.

8 Stockholm International Horse Show
The world's biggest indoor equestrian event in terms of number of spectators is held at Globen in November.

9 Bandy
This is a cross between football and ice-hockey. The bandy club Hammarby play at Zinkensdamm, on Söder.

10 Swedish Football Championship
AIK, Djurgården and Hammarby are Stockholm's major clubs. Women's football is of a very high standard and has some professional players.

Horse-racing and trotting take place throughout the winter on all-weather tracks.

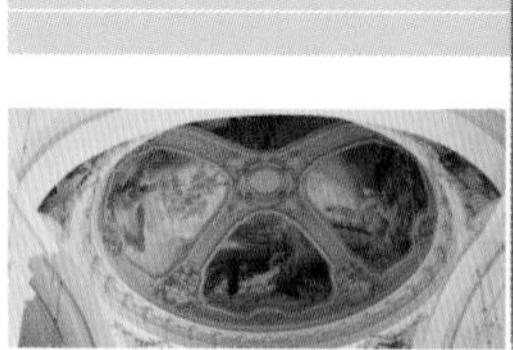

Left **Detail in dome, Adolf Fredriks Kyrka** Centre **Sculpture in Storkyrkan** Right **Riddarholmskyrkan**

Top 10 Churches

1 Tyska Kyrkan

This church is a reminder that German merchants dominated the Old Town in the Middle Ages and is also called St Gertrude's Church after the patron saint of travellers. Dating from the 17th century, it includes a gallery built in 1672 for German royals. The pulpit from 1660 is in ebony and alabaster *(see p86)*.

2 Adolf Fredriks Kyrka

Dating from 1768, this city centre church is built in the shape of a Greek cross with a central dome. The interior includes a memorial sculpture to French philosopher Descartes by Johan Tobias Sergel. The cemetery contains the grave of Prime Minister Olof Palme. *Holländargatan 16 • Map L1 • 08 20 70 76 • Open 1–7pm Mon, 10am–4pm Tue–Sun*

3 Gustav Vasa Kyrka

The Italian Neo-Baroque-style dome of this 20th-century church dominates Odenplan square. Built in 1906, its main feature is Sweden's largest Baroque sculpture, forming the altar. It was created by court sculptor Burchardt Precht between 1725 and 1731 for the Uppsala Cathedral *(see p97)*. *Odenplan • Map B2 • 08 508 886 00 • Open 11am–6pm Mon–Thu, 10am–3pm Fri, 11am–3pm Sat & Sun*

Stained-glass window of Tyska Kyrkan

4 Katarina Kyrka

Completed in 1695, Katarina Kyrka was damaged by fire in 1723 and then burnt down almost completely in 1990. It took five years to fully restore the church. Its graveyard is the resting place of famous Swedes, including assassinated foreign minister Anna Lindh. *Högbergsgatan 13 • Map D5 • 08 743 68 00 • Open 11am–5pm Mon–Fri, 10am–5pm Sat & Sun*

5 Storkyrkan

Stockholm's cathedral, with origins dating back to the 13th century, is known for its artistic treasures. The sculpture *St George and the Dragon* by Bernt Notke, from 1489, was created to mark the Battle of Brunkeberg, while the "Sun Dog Painting" of a light phenomenon over Stockholm in 1535 is said to be the oldest depiction of Stockholm in colour *(see p83)*.

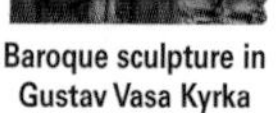

Baroque sculpture in Gustav Vasa Kyrka

6 Sofia Kyrka

Standing high up in Vitabergs park, Sofia Kyrka was completed in 1906 after Gustaf Hermansson won a contest for its design. The building has National Romantic and Gothic influences. *Vitabergsparken • Map E6 • 08 615 31 59 • Open 11am–5pm Mon–Sat, 10am–5pm Sun*

7 Engelbrektskyrkan

Dark red and imposing Engelbrektskyrkan dominates the Lärkstaden area of Östermalm, with its slim tower and the highest nave in Scandinavia supported by eight granite pillars. Opened in 1914, its interior features suitably monumental paintings by Olle Hjortzberg. *Östermalmsgatan 20B • Map D1 • 08 406 98 00 • Open 11am–3pm Tue–Sun*

8 Högalidskyrkan

This National Romantic-style church was completed in 1923. Legend has it that it was financed by two sisters, one more affluent than the other. One of the octagonal towers appears to be taller when viewed from certain angles – both towers are in fact 84 m (275 ft) high. *Högalids Kyrkväg • Map B5 • 08 616 88 00 • Open 11am–6pm Mon–Fri, 10am–4pm Sat & Sun*

9 Maria Magdalena Kyrka

With its pretty yellow spire, Maria Magdalena originated as a funeral chapel in the 14th century. The current building was completed in 1763 after a fire. Famous national poet and singer Evert Taube is buried in the churchyard. *Bellmansgatan 13 • Map D5 • 08 462 29 40 • Open 11am–5pm daily, till 3pm Wed*

Maria Magdalena Kyrka

10 Riddarholmskyrkan

The burial church for the Swedish royal family since medieval times, this is one of Stockholm's oldest buildings, parts of it dating from the 13th century. More of a museum than a church, it is only open in summer *(see p85)*.

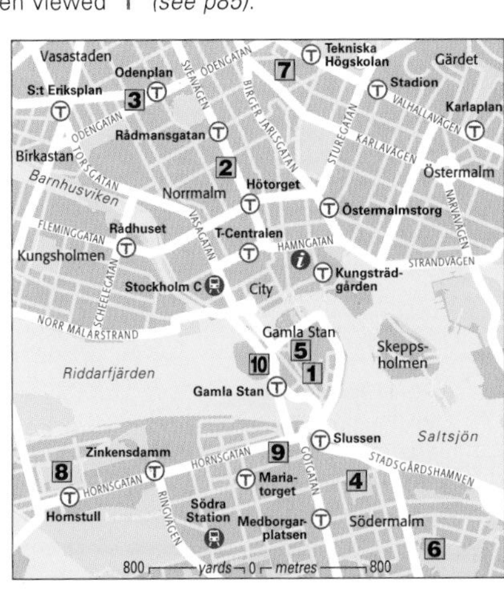

AROUND STOCKHOLM

Left **Exhibit in Medelhavsmuseet** Centre **Gallerian in Hamngatan** Right **Fruit for sale, Hötorget**

Norrmalm and City

CONSIDERED THE CENTRAL PART of town and known as the "City", much of Norrmalm was laid out in the 1960s and 70s, after a great part of its 18th-century buildings were demolished and replaced with modern high-rise blocks – a move that many people still think was hasty and ill considered. However, Norrmalm has brightened up in recent years, some areas are pedestrianized and it is now the place for affordable shopping, with many large, trendy chain stores. Of these, Åhléns City is the largest department store in Sweden, while NK is the most exclusive. The district also has some pleasant squares and the ever-popular Kungsträdgården, an urban outdoor space where there is always something going on.

Modern high-rises and flyovers in Norrmalm

TOP 10 Sights

1. Kungsgatan
2. Hötorget
3. Olof Palme's Plaque and Grave
4. Centralbadet
5. Sergels Torg
6. Kulturhuset
7. Hamngatan
8. Kungsträdgården
9. Kungliga Operan
10. Medelhavsmuseet

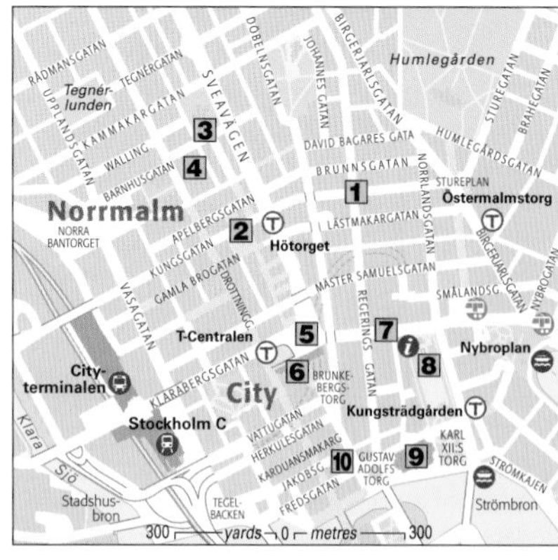

Preceding pages **Djurgårdsbron Bridge**

Busy intersection on Kungsgatan lined with shops

1 Kungsgatan

The almost dead-straight Kungsgatan, or "King's Street", was built in 1904–1905 to connect Kungsholmen, Norrmalm and Östermalm. It is notable for its two "skyscrapers", Kungstornen, built in 1924–5, and clearly modelled on the Lower Manhattan skyscrapers of that era – they were the first of their kind in Europe. Kungsgatan is a lively shopping street, with many fashion, household and electrical stores, particularly on its eastern end between Hötorget and Stureplan. *Map M2*

2 Hötorget

Just off busy Kungsgatan, lies Hötorget (Hay Market) square, a fruit and vegetable market right in the commercial heart of the city. A statue by sculptor Carl Milles stands outside the blue Royal Concert Hall (Konserthuset). To the south is Filmstaden Sergel, one of the largest multiscreen cinemas in Stockholm (international block-busters, all in original language). Beneath it is Hötorgshallen indoor market with mouthwatering displays of Swedish and foreign delicacies. To the west is the PUB department store *(see p40)*, with the latest in fashion and home furnishing, and, across the street, the Kungshallen food court *(see p66)*. *Map L2*

3 Olof Palme's Plaque and Grave

At the junction of Sveavägen and Tunnelgatan there is a memorial plaque at the spot where Swedish Prime Minister Olof Palme was assassinated on 28 February 1986. People often lay flowers here, particularly on his death anniversary. The street to the west was renamed Olof Palmes gata in his honour. Palme is buried in the nearby Adolf Fredriks Kyrka *(see p56)*, marked by a simple headstone. *Map L1*

4 Centralbadet

Located in a beautiful Art Nouveau building from 1904, Centralbadet is a relaxing oasis just off busy Drottninggatan. A swimming pool, sun roof, gym, bar, restaurant and the baths are just some of the facilities. There is also a sauna and a wide range of massages, zone therapy and facial treatments. *Drottninggatan 88 • Map L1 • 08 545 213 00 • Open 7am–9pm Mon–Fri, 9am–9pm Sat, 9am–6pm Sun • Adm • www.centralbadet.se*

Indoor swimming pool in Centralbadet

Pedestrian area, Sergels Torg

5 Sergels Torg

Although definitely not the most beautiful square in Stockholm, Sergels Torg has become an iconic landmark. It is the central hub of the city and home to the T-Centralen underground station, the only point where the red, green and blue lines intersect. The square was designed in the 1960s as part of the modernization of the entire city centre. It is known for its checkerboard pedestrian area, frequently the venue for public demonstrations and street performances. Its highlight, a glass obelisk, is stunning when lit up at night. *Map L3*

6 Kulturhuset

This cultural centre was designed by architect Peter Celsing as a "cultural living room" and has seven levels. It hosts temporary photographic and art exhibitions, films, theatre and much more. Concerts are held indoors, and, in summer, on the rooftop terrace with great views over the city. There is a café on the fifth floor and a children's library. *Sergels Torg • Map L3 • 08 508 315 08 • Opening hours vary for different sections and exhibitions • Free; adm fees for events and temporary exhibitions • www.kulturhuset.stockholm.se*

7 Hamngatan

Stretching from Sergels Torg, past Kungsträdgården and on to Berzelii Park, Hamngatan is one of Stockholm's top shopping streets. It is home to the classic NK department store *(see p40)*, trendy Gallerian *(see p40)* and the flagship H&M store *(see p41)*. Since 2010, trams are once again rolling down Hamngatan, on the number 7 line to Djurgården via Norrmalmstorg. This is also where the heritage trams *(see p77)* begin their journey to Djurgården. Norrmalmstorg is the site of the 1973 bank robbery that coined the term "Stockholm Syndrome", in which hostages start to sympathize with their captors. *Map M3*

8 Kungsträdgården

One of the most popular meeting places in the city, the "King's Garden" is a hive of activity year round. In winter, it hosts a charming Christmas market and is one of the most popular venues for ice-skating; in summer, it is a great place to simply relax. Open-air concerts and other events are held throughout the year. In 2004, 285 new linden trees replaced old and sick elm trees, and new pavilions with cafés, bars and restaurants were added. *Map M3*

Outdoor café in Kungsträdgarden

9 Kungliga Operan

The Royal Swedish Opera is the country's national stage for opera and ballet. Some productions are performed in their original language such as English, German or Italian (with Swedish subtitles). From August to May there are guided tours in English every Saturday. Take a look backstage, visit the Royal Suite and look down into the orchestra pit. *Gustav Adolf Torg 2 • Map M3 • 08 791 44 00 • www.operan.se*

Concert in progress, Kungliga Operan

10 Medelhavsmuseet

The Museum of Mediterranean and Near East Antiquities has a fine collection of ancient and historical relics from the region. The Egyptian exhibition includes mummies, mummy cases and other burial finds. The Near East and Islamic collections showcase the development of Islamic art from the 7th century onwards. The Cyprus collection is the most important of its kind outside Cyprus, comprising ancient objects excavated by the Swedish Cyprus expedition of 1927–31. The museum has a restaurant called Bagdad Café.

Fredsgatan 2 • Map M4 • 08 519 553 80 • Open noon–8pm Tue–Thu, noon–5pm Fri & Sun • Adm • www.medelhavsmuseet.se • Bagdad Café: open from 11:30am Mon–Fri; Jun–Aug: closed Mon

A Day in Norrmalm and City

Morning

Start at Kungsträdgården underground – the terminus of the blue line. It is worth a visit as it is decorated with relics from 18th-century buildings that were torn down in the 1960s. Exit at **Kungsträdgården** park; a stroll northwards through the park leads directly to **Hamngatan**, where the department store **NK** *(see p40)* sports a revolving neon clock on its roof. Carrying on up Hamngatan, there is both **Gallerian** *(see p40)* and the **H&M** flagship store *(see p41)*, before the street opens out on to **Sergels Torg**. Pop into **Kulturhuset** to check out what is on offer and for a coffee at the fifth-floor Café Panorama. Directly off Sergels Torg, pedestrianized Sergelgatan runs up to **Hötorget** *(see p61)*; grab a light lunch at **Kungshallen** *(see p66)*.

Afternoon

Not far from Hötorget is **Olof Palme's Plaque**, and his grave in Adolf Fredriks Kyrka, where there is also a memorial to French philosopher Rene Descartes who died in Stockholm in 1649, during his soujourn with Queen Kristina. **Kungsgatan** *(see p61)*, with its 1920s twin towers, has a wealth of shops, including **PUB** *(see p40)* to its west. From there, walk to **Vete-Katten** *(see p66)* for traditional *fika* (coffee and pastries). From the junction of Kungsgatan and Vasagatan, it is not far to **Cloud Nine Food and Cocktails** *(see p67)* – an excellent place for dinner.

Left **DesignTorget sign** Centre **Fragrances at Byredo** Right **Akademibokhandeln**

TOP 10 Scandinavian Design Shops

1 DesignTorget
This store has everything from kitchen items to practical but funny knick-knacks. The shop buys from designers and many items are limited editions. *Sergelgången 29 • Map L3 • 08 21 91 50*

2 Byredo
Find a favourite among the distinct scents in this fragrance house – produced in Sweden but with a nod to the founder's part-Indian heritage. *Mäster Samuelsgatan 6 • Map M2 • 08 525 026 15*

3 Design House Stockholm
A great place for unique Scandinavian designs, from furniture to fashion including tabletop items and lamps. *Smålandsgatan 11 • Map M2 • 08 509 081 13*

4 Illums Bolighus
A classic Danish interior design store that sells modern lighting, cooking, bath and wellness products. *Hamngatan 27 • Map M3 • 08 718 55 00*

5 Stockhome
Affordable smart kitchen items, coffee table books, novelties and much more are on sale in this large and colourful store. *Kungsgatan 25 • Map M2 • 08 23 08 00*

6 Brio Brand Store
This delightful children's store is famous for its high-quality, durable wooden toys. *Norrlandsgatan 18 • Map M2 • 08 611 41 10*

7 Ordning & Reda
Meaning "proper order" in Swedish, this store sells storage drawers, calendars, paper, handbags and accessories in simple, colourful designs. *Drottninggatan 82 • Map L2 • 08 10 84 96*

8 Akademibokhandeln
A huge bookstore that stocks books on Swedish history and culture along with some excellent photography books, in Swedish as well as in other languages. *Mäster Samuelsgatan 28 • Map M2 • 01 074 411 00*

9 Lagerhaus
Many of the modern and reasonably priced home accessories that Lagerhaus stocks are its own designs – around 50 per cent are exclusive and can only be found in its own stores. *Drottninggatan 31 • Map L3 • 08 23 72 00*

10 Norrgavel
Home furnishings and accessories in this eco-friendly store are designed by Swedish designer Nirvan Richter in clean, minimalist style. *Birger Jarlsgatan 27 • Map M1 • 08 545 220 50*

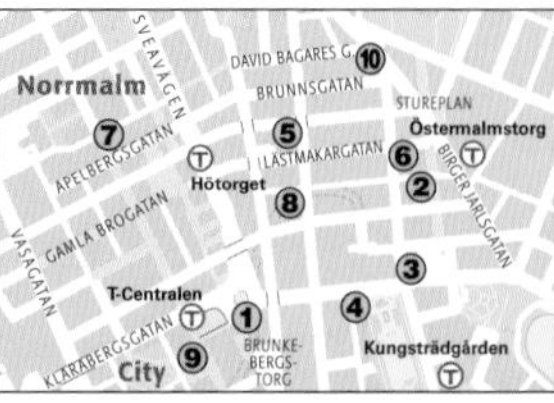

Most big downtown stores are open seven days a week.

Left **Fashion store Gina Tricot** Right **Caps on display at WeSC**

Top 10 Fashion Shops

1 Acne

This is the flagship store of a brand that has become famous for its trendy and innovative collection of jeans. It sells quality clothing. *Norrmalmstorg 2 • Map M2 • 08 611 64 11 • www.acnestudios.com*

2 Hope

Designs in this store are influenced by classic, vintage and timeless styles. *Norrlandsgatan 12 • Map M2 • 08 678 11 30 • www.hope-sthlm.com*

3 Marc by Marc Jacobs

This is a Swedish flagship store for globally successful American fashion designer Marc Jacobs. *Smålandsgatan 10 • Map M2 • 08 660 01 70 • www.marcjacobs.com*

4 Whyred

With strong connections to fashion in contemporary music and art, Whyred is urban clothing based around mod, beatnik and indie. It has even been described as the "Indie super label". *Mäster Samuelsgatan 5 • Map M2 • 08 679 58 60 • www.whyred.se*

5 Rodebjer

Swedish designer Carin Rodebjer's clothing for women has won many awards, including Elle Fashion Designer of the Year three times. The clothes are both elegant and challenging, with influences ranging from Swedish folk to 1920s Paris. *Jakobsbersgatan 6 • Map M2 • 08 410 460 95 • www.rodebjer.com*

6 COS

Collection of Style (COS) is a spin-off from H&M – high-end fashion at an affordable price. The style is typically Swedish – modern with a retro touch. *Biblioteksgatan 3 • Map M2 • 08 545 010 50 • www.cosstores.com*

7 Gina Tricot

A widely successful women's fashion brand, Gina Tricot boasts low prices and constant innovation. *Hamngatan 10 • Map M3 • 08 23 43 50 • www.ginatricot.com*

8 WeSC

A street fashion brand, WeAretheSuperlativeConspiracy (WeSC) has bold, urban and easy-to-wear styles. It also offers a fantastic range of high-quality cool headphones. *Kungsgatan 66 • Map M2 • 08 21 25 15 • www.wesc.com*

9 Tiger of Sweden

Though founded in 1903, Tiger of Sweden is anything but old-fashioned. It emphasizes quality, clean-cut designs with attitude. *Jakobsbersgatan 8 • Map M2 • 08 440 30 60 • www.tigerofsweden.com*

10 Solo

This shop stocks almost every make of jeans imaginable – over 40 different brands – including leading Swedish and international names. *Smålandsgatan 20 • Map M2 • 08 545 000 30 • www.soloblogg.se*

Shops usually close at 7pm on weekdays.

Left **Fresh breads, Vete-Katten** Centre **Kungshallen's outdoor area** Right **Pizzas at Pizza Hatt**

TOP 10 Cafés, Pubs and Bars

1 Sosta

This Italian-style café bar is consistently raved about by those for whom an espresso is serious business. *Jakobsbergsatan 5 • Map M2 • 08 611 71 07 • Open 8am–6pm Mon–Fri, 10am–5pm Sat*

2 Glenn Miller Café

Food is French themed with lots of options for mussels at this cozy jazz pub. *Brunnsgatan 21a • Map M1 • 08 10 03 22 • Open 11am–3pm and 5pm–1am Mon–Thu, 11am–3pm and 5pm–2am Fri, 5pm–2am Sat; Sun (only when live music): 6pm–1am*

3 KGB

This pub is designed around a "Soviet nostalgia" theme – order a vodka, or a Russian beer. It also hosts club nights. *Malmskillnadsgatan 45 • Map L2 • 08 20 91 55 • Open 5–11pm Mon–Tue, 5pm–midnight Wed–Thu, 4pm–2am Fri, 5pm–2am Sat*

4 Vete-Katten

An old-fashioned café opened in 1928, the "wheat cat" features traditional cakes and buns amidst lace cloths and white china. *Kungsgatan 55 • Map K2 • 08 20 84 05 • Open 7:30am–7:30pm Mon–Fri, 9:30am–5pm Sat*

5 Kåken

An American-style, trendy bar, this is a good place for an early evening drink as it gets busy with the after-work crowd. *Regeringsgatan 66 • Map M2 • 08 20 60 10 • Open 6pm–2am Wed–Sat*

6 Kungshallen

The only food court in Stockholm has different counters in one seating area; the floor above has four types of restaurant-cafés. It is a good choice for a cheap sit-down meal. *Kungsgatan 44 • Map L2 • 07 086 556 20 • Open 9am–11pm Mon–Fri, 11am–11pm Sat, noon–11pm Sun*

7 Monks Café and Brewery

Not only does this pub stock an extraordinary range of beers, it also brews its own. *Sveavägen 39 • Map K1 • 08 24 13 10*

8 Pizza Hatt

This quirky place serves great sourdough pizzas using only fresh ingredients. Eat in or take away. *Upplandsgatan 9 • Map K1 • Open 1am–9pm Tue–Sun*

9 Bianchi Café & Cycles

It is all about traditional Italian quality in this café and bicycle shop serving excellent coffee and snacks. *Norrlandsgatan 20 • Map M2 • 08 611 21 00 • Open 7:30am–7pm Mon–Wed, 7:30am–9pm Thu–Fri, 11am–9pm Sat, 11:30am–5pm Sun*

10 Café Panorama

Have lunch or coffee in this café on the fifth floor of Kulturhuset *(see p62)*. Café Panorama has great views over the city from its huge windows. *Map L3 • 08 21 10 35 • Open 11am–10pm Tue–Fri, 11am–6pm Sat, 11am–5pm Sun*

All bars and nightclubs in Sweden must have a food menu by law.

Price Categories

For a three-course meal for one with half a bottle of wine (or equivalent meal), taxes and extra charges.

Ⓚ	400–550 kr
ⓀⓀ	550–700 kr
ⓀⓀⓀ	700–1000 kr
ⓀⓀⓀⓀ	over 1000 kr

Left **Tasty food at Tjabba Thai**

TOP 10 Places to Eat

1 Operakällarens Bakficka

Located in Operakällaren, "Bakfickan" or "hip pocket" is a place to enjoy old-time Swedish favourites such as meatballs. *Karl XII:s Torg • Map M3 • 08 676 58 00 • Open 11:30am–11pm Mon–Fri, noon–10pm Sat •* ⓀⓀ

2 Wedholms Fisk

Traditional, classy fish restaurant that offers great choice. *Nybrokajen 17 • Map N3 • 08 611 78 74 • Open 11:30am–2pm & 6pm–11pm Mon, 11:30am–11pm Tue–Fri, 5pm–11pm Sat •* ⓀⓀⓀ

3 Zink Grill

A French bistro that serves breakfast, lunch and dinner. *Biblioteksgatan 5 • Map N3 • 08 611 42 22 • Open 8am–10:30pm Mon–Fri, 1pm–1am Sat–Sun •* ⓀⓀⓀ

4 F12

This Michelin-starred restaurant continues to win awards for its modern take on classic cuisine. *Fredsgatan 12 • Map L4 • 08 505 244 04 • Open 11:30am–2pm & 5pm–1am Mon–Fri, 5pm–1am Sat •* ⓀⓀⓀⓀ

5 Supper

Various South American flavours dominate the dishes here, which are meant to be shared. *Tegnérgatan 37 • Map K1 • 08 23 24 24 • Open 5pm–midnight Mon–Tue, 5pm–1am Wed–Sat •* ⓀⓀ

6 Cloud Nine Food and Cocktails

Relaxed French atmosphere and an outdoor plaza in summer. *Torsgatan 1 • Map J2 • 08 653 69 90 • Lunch: 11:30am–2:30pm Mon–Fri; Dinner: 5–10pm Mon–Wed, 5pm–midnight Thu–Sat •* ⓀⓀ

7 Nalen Restaurang

Serves classic Swedish food. *Regeringsgatan 74 • Map M1 • 08 505 292 01 • Open 11:30am–11pm Mon–Fri, 5–11pm Sat •* ⓀⓀ

8 Belgobaren

Mussels are served in 14 ways, from classic *moules frites* to those with Asian curry sauces. *Bryggargatan 12a • Map K3 • 08 24 66 40 • Open 11–1am Mon–Fri, 1pm–1am Sat, 2pm–1am Sun •* Ⓚ

9 Tjabba Thai

Some of the city's best Thai food is served here, including a very good seafood selection. *Wallingatan 7 • Map K1 • 08 21 99 88 • Open 11am–10pm Mon–Fri •* Ⓚ

10 San Leandro Tapas

Cheerful and colourful, San Leandro Tapas boasts an extensive tapas menu, with many good options for vegetarians. *Sveavägen 74 • Map L1 • 08 612 24 30 • Lunch: 11:30am–2pm; Dinner: 4–10pm Tue–Thu, Fri 11:30am–11pm, Sat 2–11pm •* Ⓚ

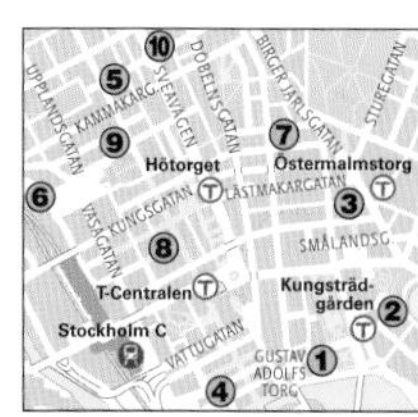

Left **Shaded walkway along Mälarpromenaden** Right **Old telescope at the Observatoriemuseet**

Kungsholmen and Vasastan

ONCE KNOWN AS "FAMINE ISLAND", *with grim industrial businesses and cramped housing, Kungsholmen began to improve in the early 20th century when its best-known landmark, the City Hall, was built, followed by elegant waterfront houses along Norr Mälarstrand. It became a major residential area; the underground green line arrived in 1952 and today it offers a pleasant alternative to the city centre, with a good variety of shops and cafés. Nearby Vasastan, developed in the late 19th century to accommodate the rising population, is home to the lively area around Odengatan, with restaurants, bars and nightclubs as well as the iconic City Library and the popular Vasaparken.*

Mälarpromenaden along Norr Mälarstrand on Kungsholmen

Top 10 Sights

1. Norr Mälarstrand
2. Rålambhovsparken
3. Stadshuset
4. Sven-Harrys (Konstmuseum)
5. Vasaparken
6. Strindbergsmuseet
7. Observatoriemuseet
8. Sveavägen
9. Stadsbiblioteket
10. Judiska Museet

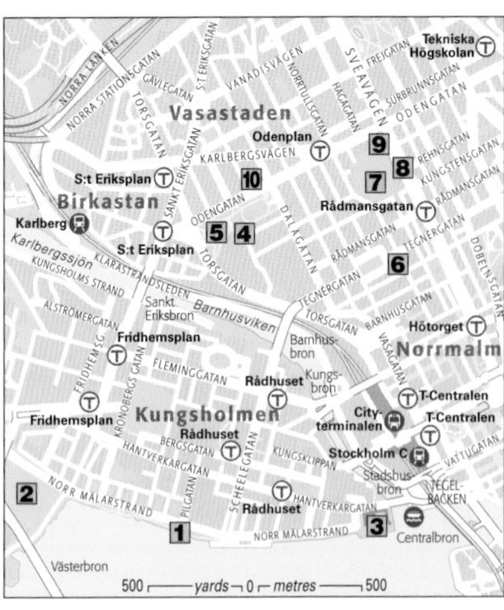

1 Norr Mälarstrand

The walk along Norr Mälarstrand is picturesque and popular. Its quay, lined with old ships and houseboats, transforms into a waterside footpath in its western stretch. Either start at Stadshuset or walk towards it from Västerbron (Bus 4 stops at Västerbroplan; take the steps down into Rålambshov park to pick up the shoreline walk). Along the way there are several good stops for refreshments and food, as well as panoramic views across Riddarfjärden towards Söder. *Map J4*

The imposing Stadshuset

2 Rålambhovsparken

Known locally as "Rålis", this was created as a functional park in 1936, the same time that Västerbron was built. It is a popular summer haunt with sunbathers, as well as football, *brännboll (see p55)* or frisbee players. An open-air theatre was opened here in 1953. *Map A3*

Rålambhovsparken seen from Västerbron

Shopping on Kungsholmen

Kungsholmen is a great shopping alternative to the city centre crowds. St Eriksgatan and Fleminggatan are the main shopping streets while Fridhemsgatan and Hantverkargatan are good for second hand shops.

3 Stadshuset

With its dramatic waterside setting on Riddarfjärden, the City Hall is visible from far away, and one of the most famous landmarks in Stockholm. Opened in 1923, it is built from 8 million bricks in the National Romantic style and is home to Stockholm's municipal council *(see pp16–17)*.

4 Sven-Harrys (Konstmuseum)

Building contractor and art collector Sven-Harrys built this spectacular, six-storeyed, brass and blonde-wood building to house an art museum, exhibition galleries and restaurants as well as private apartments. The recessed penthouse is a replica of his own 18th-century mansion and displays his art collection. Do not miss the rooftop sculpture garden. *Eastmansvägen 10 • Map B2 • 08 511 600 60 • Open 11am–7pm Wed–Fri; 11am–5pm Sat & Sun, closed Mon & Tue • www.sven-harrys.se*

For a fantastic view of Stockholm, walk up across Västerbron.

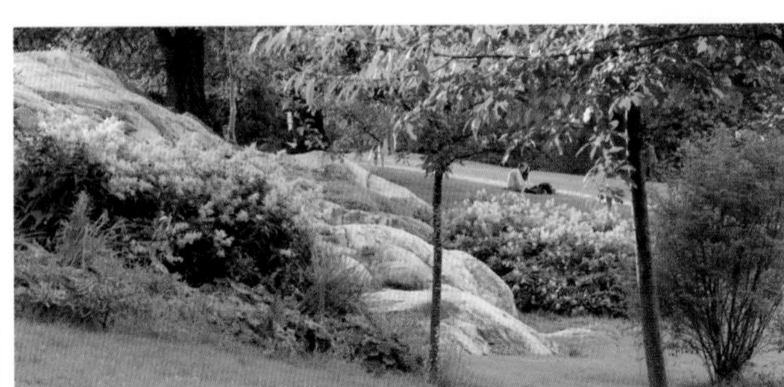

Undulating green landscape of Vasaparken

5 Vasaparken

Vasastan's green lung was developed in the early 20th century as an "open place for free games" – a role it retains today with football pitches, *boule* courts, a landscaped playground and an ice-skating rink in winter. There are also large grassy areas and terraced walks. In 1917, *Arbetaren* (The Worker), a statue by Gottfrid Larsson, was erected to honour the working class. Kiosks sell snacks. *Map B2*

6 Strindbergsmuseet

Considered the father of modern Swedish literature, and also a prolific artist, August Strindberg lived in what he called the "Blue Tower" for the last four years of his life. The house is faithfully preserved as he left it, and Strindberg's study, living room and bedroom take the visitor back to 1912. There are also many photographic portraits of Strindberg and his family, as well as photographs of places associated with him.

Drottninggatan 85 • Map C2 • 08 411 53 54 • Open noon–4pm Tue–Sun; Jul–Aug: 10am–4pm • Adm • www.strindbergsmuseet.se

Signage outside entrance to Strindbergsmuseet

7 Observatoriemuseet

During the 18th and 19th centuries, the old astronomical observatory conducted research in the fields of astronomy, meteorology and geography. Closed over 1929–30, it reopened in 1991 and efforts to re-create some of the rooms with their instruments are ongoing.

Drottninggatan 120 • Map C2 • 08 545 483 90 • Open 6–9pm Tue & Thu (Oct–Mar), observation every half hour; 12–3pm Sun • Book in advance for guided tours for groups in English • Adm • www.observatoriet.kva.se

8 Sveavägen

Broad, straight and linking the city centre with Odenplan and beyond, Sveavägen is built like a Parisian boulevard. After an unpromising start at Sergels Torg, the street comes into its own after Hötorget – tree-lined and with upmarket shops and many restaurants. Adolf Fredriks Kyrka *(see p56)* and the Stadsbiblioteket are here. After Odenplan, it becomes more tranquil, ending on the city's northern fringes, just a short walk from Hagaparken *(see pp28–9)*.

9 Stadsbiblioteket

The City Library is one of the most influential buildings constructed in Stockholm in the early 20th century. Opened in 1928, it was designed by Gunnar Asplund in the so-called Nordic Classicist style. Painted in eye-catching pale orange, its highlight is the central rotunda. Inside, packed bookshelves cover the walls of its tiered balconies, yet with its tall white ceiling, the rotunda seems well lit. It was the first library in Sweden to adopt the principle of open shelves where books could be accessed without help from the library staff. *Sveavägen 73 • Map C1 • 08 508 310 60 • Open 9am–9pm Mon–Thu, 9am–7pm Fri, noon–4pm Sat–Sun • www.biblioteket.stockholm.se*

Interior of Stadsbiblioteket's rotunda

10 Judiska Museet

The Jewish museum features unique objects linked to the religion and history of Jews in Sweden. Spiritual artifacts include the *Torah* – the five books of Moses – and a collection of eight-stemmed *chanukis* or candlesticks. The museum depicts the history of Jews in Sweden since Aaron Isaac became the first Jewish immigrant to settle in Sweden in 1774. *Hälsingegatan 2 • Map B2 • 08 31 01 43 • Open noon–4pm Sun–Fri • Adm • www.judiska-museet.se*

A Day in Kungsholmen and Vasastan

Morning

Start off at **Stadshuset** *(see pp16–17)*: tours start at around 10am and the tower is open from 9:15am from May to September. From Stadshuset take the lovely waterside walk along Norr Mälarstrand – perhaps pop into **Petite France** *(see p72)* for morning coffee and a pastry. St Eriksgatan starts at the northeastern corner of **Rålambshovparken** *(see p69)* and goes right through the main shopping area of Kungsholmen. As well as taking in the shops, including the mall at Fridhemsplan, grab a light lunch at Café Fix at St Eriksgatan 35, said to be Stockholm's oldest café.

Afternoon

Crossing St Eriksbron leads to the northern end of St Eriksgatan with its cluster of record stores. From here it is a very short walk to **Vasaparken**, a lovely park to put your feet up with an ice cream in the summer or try ice-skating in winter. Old-fashioned **Konditori Ritorno** *(see p72)* is right opposite the park: cosy and warm in winter and with a sunny outdoor area in the summer. Head on to Odenplan and pop into the **Stadsbiblioteket** (library) to admire its impressive rotunda. Stadsbiblioteket lends more than a million books every year. Round off the day with dinner at **Cafe Tranan** *(see p72)*: eat in the restaurant or the bar, before enjoying an after-dinner drink with the local crowd.

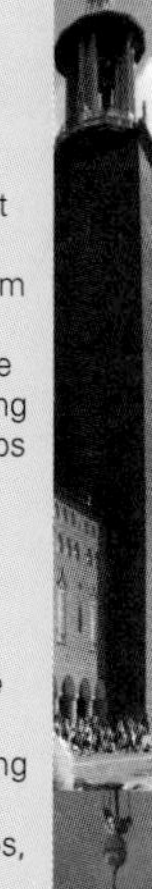

Left **Pastries in Konditori Ritorno** Right **Outdoor seats, Vurma**

TOP 10 Cafés, Pubs and Bars

1 Café Tranan
A timeless classic, this basement bar is the perfect place to blend in with the locals. *Karlbergsvägen 14 • Map B1 • 08 527 281 00 • Open 5pm–midnight Mon–Thu, 5pm–1am Fri–Sat, 5pm–1am Sun*

2 Konditori Ritorno
Order your choice of cake from the bakery in the front and then pour your own coffee in the dark, roomy, windowless café. *Odengatan 80–82 • Map B2 • 08 32 01 06 • Open 7am–8pm Mon–Thu, 7am–6pm Fri, 10am–6pm Sat*

3 Konditori Valand
An original, this café has remained unchanged since it opened in 1954, with wooden walls, matching furniture and an old cash register. *Surbrunnsgatan 48 • Map C1 • 08 30 04 76 • Open 8am–7pm Mon–Fri, 9am–5pm Sat*

4 Man in the Moon
This traditional pub with an English feel serves different and unusual types of Swedish beer. *Tegnérgatan 2 C • Map C2 • 08 458 95 00 • Open 11am–11pm Mon, 11am–midnight Tue–Thu, 11–1am Fri, 1pm–1am Sat*

5 Non Solo Bar
Highly rated for its coffee, this Italian café serves classic food such as pasta, salads and sandwiches. *Odengatan 34 • Map C1 • 08 440 20 82 • Open 7am–8pm Mon–Fri, 9am–6pm Sat–Sun*

6 Lemon Bar
With lots of dancing and hits from the 1980s, this small bar, with no pretensions, is a happy place to be. *Scheelegatan 8 • Map B3 • 08 650 17 78 • Open 5pm–1am Tue, 5pm–3am Wed–Sat*

7 Vurma
This cafe offers a great selection of grilled sandwiches with names such as "Alien", "Freak" and "Clown". *Gästrikegatan 2 • Map B2 • 08 30 62 30 • Open 9am–6pm Mon–Sat, 10am–6pm Sun*

8 Orangeriet
Located by the seafront at Norr Mälarstrand, this is a weekend café by day and bar at night. *Norr Mälarstrand Kajplats 464 • Map B4 • 08 505 244 75 • Café: open 11am–4pm Sat, 11am–6pm Sun; Bar: open 4pm–1am Mon–Fri, noon-1am Sat, noon- midnight Sun*

9 Olssons Video
Dark and intimate, this club is stylishly decorated with bar stools and leather seats. Music is classic club sounds. *Odengatan 41 • Map C1 • 08 673 38 00 • Open 9pm–3am Wed–Sat*

10 Petite France
Entering this café feels like stepping into a traditional French bakery, with bread and pastries to match. It is open for breakfast and lunch. *John Ericssonsgatan 6 • Map B3 • 08 618 28 00 • Open 8am–6pm Tue–Fri, 9am–5pm Sat–Sun*

Most regular daytime cafés are not licensed.

Price Categories

For a three-course meal for one with half a bottle of wine (or equivalent meal), taxes and extra charges.

Kr	400–550 kr
KrKr	550–700 kr
KrKrKr	700–1000 kr
KrKrKrKr	over 1000 kr

Left **Nostalgic restaurant Tennstopet**

TOP 10 Places to Eat

1 Linguini

Cosy Linguini serves good Italian food. Book in advance as there are only around 10 tables. *Frejgatan 48 • Map B1 • 08 31 49 15 • Open 5–9pm Mon–Tue; 5–10pm Wed–Fri, 4:30–10pm Sat • KrKr*

2 Claes på Hörnet

"Claes on the corner" claims to be Sweden's oldest inn, dating from 1731. Book ahead. *Surbrunnsgatan 20 • Map C1 • 08 16 51 36 • 5pm–midnight Sat & Mon, 11:30am–midnight Tue–Fri • KrKr*

3 Svartengrens

This meat restaurant serves ecologically sourced food and is also famous for its cocktails. *Tulegatan 24 • Map C1 • 08 612 65 50 • 5pm–1am Tue–Sun • KrKrKr*

4 Grill

Grilled food from around the world and madly eclectic interiors. *Drottninggatan 89 • Map C2 • 08 31 45 30 • Open 11:15am–2pm & 5pm–1am Mon–Fri, 4pm–1am Sat, 3–11pm Sun • KrKrKr*

5 Restaurang Malaysia

The full-flavoured Malaysian dishes here include many vegetarian options. *Luntmakargatan 98 • Map C2 • 08 673 56 69 • Lunch: open 11am–2:30pm Mon–Fri; Dinner: open 5–10pm Mon–Thu, 5–11pm Fri–Sat, 4–9pm Sun • Kr*

6 Tennstopet

Relive the 1940s and 1950s in this place serving Swedish food. *Dalagatan 50 • Map B2 • 08 32 25 18 • 4pm–1am Mon–Fri; 1pm–1am Sat–Sun • Bar food: KrKr • Restaurant: KrKrKr*

7 Restaurang Jonas

Go for the full tasting menu at this award winning restaurant, or à la carte in the bar. *Flemminggatan 39 • Map B3 • 08 650 22 20 • Open 6–11pm Tue–Sat • KrKr*

8 Restaurang Lux

This Michelin-starred restaurant offers seasonal cooking with locally sourced fresh produce. *Primusgatan 116 • 08 619 01 90 • Open 11:30am–2pm & 6–11pm Tue–Fri, 5–11pm Sat • KrKrKr*

9 Trattorian

Italian cuisine is served on a waterside pontoon. *Norr Mälarstrand 9, Kajplats 464 • Map B4 • 08 505 244 50 • Open 5pm–1am Mon–Sat, 5pm–midnight Sun • KrKr*

10 El Diablo

Even though it has Europe's largest tequila assortment, with over 100 varieties, El Diablo is a restaurant and not a bar. The menus change regularly. *Norra Agnegatan 43 • Map B3 • 08 650 50 69 • Open 5pm–midnight Mon–Thu, 5pm–1am Fri–Sat, 4pm–midnight Sun • KrKrKr*

Left **Port side of the *Vasa*** Right **Lemur at Skansen**

Östermalm and Djurgården

ALTHOUGH NEIGHBOURS, ÖSTERMALM AND DJURGÅRDEN offer contrasting experiences. Östermalm is the most exclusive part of the city, and is home to the most expensive restaurants and designer shops. Djurgården, on the other hand, is largely tranquil – it has only 800 permanent residents and is part of the Stockholm National City Park. Most of its eastern part is mainly undisturbed parkland with excellent walks, while the western part is packed with attractions drawing visitors and locals alike – Skansen, Junibacken, Vasamuseet and Gröna Lund funfair.

TOP 10 Sights

1. Stureplan
2. Humlegården
3. Historiska Museet
4. Strandvägen
5. Tram rides
6. Walk along Djurgårdsbrunnsviken
7. Gröna Lund
8. Skansen
9. Vasamuseet
10. Nordiska Museet

Geese at Galärparken, Djurgården

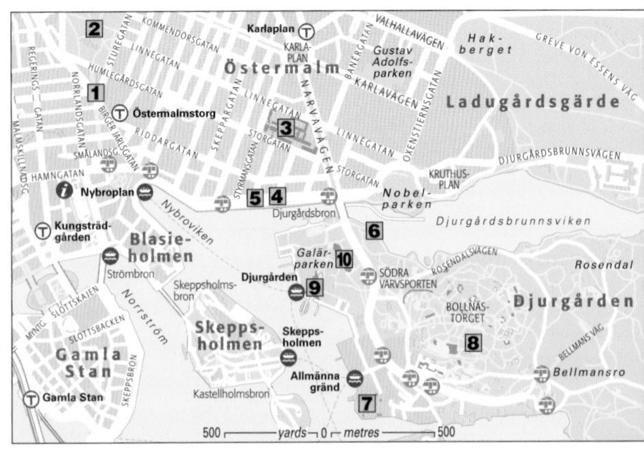

1 Stureplan

Originally just the name of a square with a quirky mushroom-shaped rain shelter at its heart, "Stureplan" has become synonymous with luxury and style. On the streets radiating from it are exclusive fashion houses, expensive restaurants, bars and nightclubs. *Map M2*

2 Humlegården

Just a stone's throw away from Stureplan, the broad oak tree-lined paths and extensive lawns park of Humlegården, or "Hop Garden," are a welcome retreat from the busy city centre. This former royal garden has been a public park since 1869, boasting a large play area and, in summer, outdoor clubs and bars. A statue of Swedish naturalist Carl Linnaeus looks out over the middle of the park. Humlegården is also home to the National Library of Sweden. *Map M1*

Statue of Carl Linnaeus in Humlegården

3 Historiska Museet

Sweden's National Historical Museum opened in 1943. On display are collections from Prehistory through the Viking era to the Middle Ages. Fantastic artifacts include ancient gold jewellery, while a reconstruction

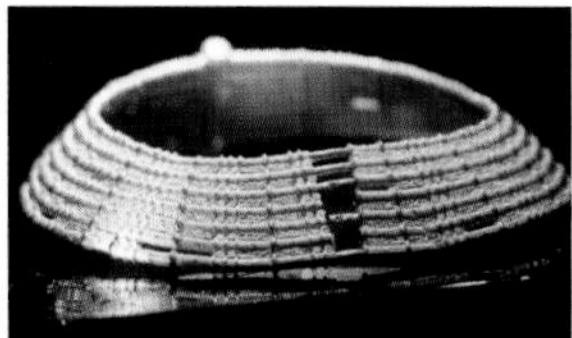

Gold necklace, Historiska Museet

shows what a small rural church looked like in Västergötland at the end of the Middle Ages. Discover how people lived, worked and ate in prehistoric times; view priceless artifacts that were unearthed after 3,000 years. The Viking exhibitions reveal how these people were mainly peaceful traders and not brutal robbers *(see pp26–7)*.

4 Strandvägen

Completed in time for Stockholm's World Fair in 1897, Strandvägen is one of the most prestigious streets in the city. Running almost parallel to the waterside of Nybroviken, the wide boulevard has an air of old grandeur, particularly when the vintage trams are rattling along. Bünsowska Huset, at No. 29–33, designed by architects Isak Gustaf Clason and Anders Gustaf Forsberg, sets the standard for the street. The tree-lined middle of the street shades walking and cycling lanes. *Map P3*

Östermalm – Stockholm's exclusive district

Östermalm was developed in the late 19th century around the wide boulevards of Strandvägen, Karlavägen, Narvavägen and Valhallavägen. Some of the best architects of the era shaped the district in a Renaissance style. Östermalm is also home to the diplomatic quarter – many embassies are housed here.

Roller coasters in Gröna Lund amusement park

5 Tram rides

A charming way to see Djurgården's attractions is in an old tramcar. Starting at Norrmalmstorg, the trams run along Strandvägen before swinging across the bridge into Djurgården, passing Skansen and Gröna Lund and on to Waldemarsudde art gallery. The most popular is the café tram, which serves tea, coffee or a soft drink with a bun during the journey; check the timetable as several other vintage trams as well as new, high-tech ones traffic this route. *Late-Apr–mid-Jun: 11am–7pm Sat, Sun & public hols; late-Jun–late-Aug: 11am–7pm daily; late-Aug–mid-Dec: 11am–5pm Sat, Sun & public hols • www.sparvagssallskapet.se*

6 Walk along Djurgårdsbrunnsviken

Alight from the bus or tram at Djurgårdsbron, opposite Nordiska Museet. Walk through the bright blue gates to pick up the path along Rosendalsvägen, by the water's edge, and watch gleaming mahogany boats, canoes and pedalos glide past. The path leads to the biodynamic market garden and café at Rosendals Trädgård *(see p78)*. *Map R4*

7 Gröna Lund

By the waterfront on Djurgården, Gröna Lund is both an amusement park and a major concert venue. The funfair features 32 attractions, including seven roller coasters and the world's highest Free Fall Tilt. First opened in the 1880s, the park also includes charming vintage carousels and sideshows. There are numerous restaurants, bars and fast food outlets *(see pp22–3)*.

8 Skansen

Located in a beautiful hilly spot on Djurgården, Skansen is deservedly one of the city's most enduring attractions. Journey through Sweden over the ages, or visit Stockholm's only zoo with animals native to Scandinavia such as elk, bears, lynx and wolves. Visit the town district with wooden urban dwellings and crafts such as

Canalside path along Djurgårdsbrunnsviken

glass blowing and printing. There is also a terrarium, a monkey house and a zoo for children as well as gentle rides *(see pp8–9)*.

9 Vasamuseet

Getting up close to the *Vasa*, the only preserved 17th-century ship in the world, is a unique and memorable experience. Built as the jewel of the Swedish fleet, she sank just minutes into its maiden voyage from Stockholm in 1628, and lay undisturbed for 333 years. In 1961, an extraordinary salvage operation raised the ship – different exhibitions inside the Vasamuseet describe the story of the vessel and its painstaking restoration *(see pp10–11)*.

Folk costumes, Nordiska Museet

10 Nordiska Museet

With a huge number of exhibits, Nordiska Museet comprehensively charts everyday life in Sweden from the 16th century to the present day. Exhibitions focus on periods of major change and transition – fashion trends are explored from the 1780s, 1860s and 1960s, interiors cover both the elaborate styles of the 19th century and the practical considerations of the housing boom of the 1970s. Find out how Swedish traditions such as dancing around the Midsummer pole originated *(see pp24–5)*.

A Day in Östermalm and Djurgården

Morning

Start off like thousands of people do at the concrete "mushroom" right on **Stureplan** *(see p75)*. Directly behind is **Sturegallerian** *(see p41)*, an ideal place to shop for exclusive brands or browse the excellent Hedengrens bookshop which stocks books in many languages. There are also several cafés to choose from for morning coffee – the cosy Le Café is recommended. Next, head for the shopping heart of Östermalm in the streets leading off Östermalmstorg. Drop by the 19th-century food hall, **Östermalms Saluhall** *(see p40)*. From there, it is a short walk to **Brasserie Elverket** *(see p79)* on Linnégatan – an excellent choice for lunch on weekdays with several good-value dishes of the day.

Afternoon

Burn off the calories by strolling down to **Strandvägen** *(see p75)*; either continue along the lovely waterside boulevard, or hop on to a bus or tram – a vintage one if it is running – to **Djurgården**. Alight at **Skansen** *(see pp8–9)* and set aside an entire afternoon to visit its old town, Scandinavian zoo and the children's fairground attractions. Round off the day with a classic Swedish dinner at **Ulla Windbladh** *(see p43)*. If it is booked, the nearby **Villa Godthem** *(see p79)* is a good option; both have outdoor seating in summer.

Left **Sturehof's outdoor tables** Right **Cinnamon rolls in Saturnus**

Top 10 Cafés, Pubs and Bars

1 Rosendals Trädgård
This idyllic garden café sells home-made organic salads, soups, sandwiches and pastries. *Rosendalsterrassen 12 • Map G4 • 08 545 812 70 • Open 11am–5pm Mon–Fri, 11am–6pm Sat & Sun • www.rosendalstradgard.se*

2 Blå Porten
Close to Gröna Lund, Skansen and Vasamuseet, Blå Porten offers a wide self-service menu. *Djurgårdsvägen 64 • Map R5 • 08 663 87 59 • Open11am–10pm Mon–Fri, 11am–7pm Sat & Sun*

3 Sturekatten
The "Sture cat" is an old-fashioned tea and coffee house in an apartment building from the 1700s. *Riddargatan 4 • Map N2 • 08 611 16 12 • Open 9am–7pm Mon–Fri, 10am–6pm Sat, 11am–6pm Sun*

4 Riche
A classic meeting place with several bars. *Birger Jarlsgatan 4 • Map N2 • 08 545 035 60 • Open 7:30am–midnight Mon, 7:30am–2am Tue–Fri, noon–2am Sat, noon–midnight Sun*

5 East
East serves Asian food by day, and turns into a nightclub after 11pm. *Stureplan 13 • Map M2 • 08 611 49 59 • Open 11:30–3am Mon–Fri, 5pm–3am Sat & Sun*

6 Obaren (Sturehof)
Central to Stureplan's busy club scene, Obaren is a good choice for those who just want to party. *Sturegallerian 42, Stureplan 2 • Map M2 • 08 440 57 30 • Open 5pm–2am Fri, 7pm–2am all other nights*

7 Hotellet
With one of Stockholm's longest bars, specializing in cocktails, Hotellet has an outdoor bar in summer, making it the only "nightlife garden" in the city centre. *Linnégatan 18 • Map N1 • 08 442 89 00 • Open 11:30am–midnight Mon & Tue, 11:30–1am Wed, 11:30–2am Thu–Fri, 6pm–2am Sat*

8 Valhallabageriet
New sourdough bakeries seem to spring up every week in Stockholm, but Valhallabageriet has endured. It also serves good coffee. *Valhallavägen 174 • Map R1 • 08 662 97 63 • Open 7am–6pm Mon–Fri, 8am–1pm Sat*

9 Saturnus
This café and lunch spot inspired by France serves big bowls of coffee with cinnamon rolls to match. It also serves breakfast and brunch and offers its customers international newspapers to read. *Eriksbergsgatan 6 • Map D2 • 08 611 77 00 • Open 8am–8pm Mon–Fri, 9am–7pm Sat–Sun*

10 Tudor Arms
The Tudor Arms has been open since 1969 and feels genuinely British. *Grevgatan 31 • Map P2 • 08 660 27 12 • Open 11:30am–11pm Mon–Fri, 1–11pm Sat, 1–7pm Sun*

Lunch dishes of the day, "Dagens rätt", are always much cheaper than the à la carte menu.

Price Categories

For a three-course meal for one with half a bottle of wine (or equivalent meal), taxes and extra charges.		
	Kr	400–550 kr
	KrKr	550–700 kr
	KrKrKr	700–1000 kr
	KrKrKrKr	over 1000 kr

Left **Ulla Winbladh** Right **Table setting in Teatergrillen**

TOP 10 Places to Eat

1 Villa Godthem

Located in a 19th-century house set in parkland, Villa Godthem serves classic Swedish dishes. *Rosendalsvägen 9 • Map R4 • 08 505 244 15 • Lunch: 11:30am–2pm Mon–Fri, noon–3pm Sat; Dinner: 5–10pm Mon–Fri, 4–10pm Sat & Sun • KrKrKr*

2 Ulla Winbladh

A traditional historic Swedish inn, it is located in the park just after Djurgårdsbron. Book ahead. *Rosendalsvägen 8 • Map R4 • 08 534 897 01 • Open 11:30am–10pm Mon, 11:30am–11pm Tue–Fri, noon–11pm Sat, noon–10pm Sun • KrKrKr*

3 Sturehof

This modern yet classical restaurant in Östermalm specializes in seafood. *Stureplan 2 • Map M2 • 08 440 57 30 • Open 11–2am Mon–Fri, noon–2am Sat, 1pm–2am Sun • KrKrKr*

4 PA & Co

Swedish food with a twist. Book ahead. *Riddargatan 8 • Map N2 • 08 611 08 45 • Open 5pm–midnight daily • KrKrKr*

5 Cassi

Go back to the 1970s in this family-run bistro. *Narvavägen 30 • Map Q2 • 08 661 74 61 • Open 10:45am–8pm Mon–Fri, 1–8pm Sun • KrKr*

6 Bistro Nouveau

This incredibly inviting, perfectly decorated bistro offers a small classic French menu. *Kommendörsgatan 7 • Map N1 • 08 661 42 42 • Open 5–11pm Tue–Wed; 5pm–1am Thu–Sat, 4–9pm Sun • KrKr*

7 Teatergrillen

Very pricey French-Swedish crossover restaurant. *Nybrogatan 3 • Map N2 • 08 545 035 65 • Open Lunch: 11:30am–2:30pm Mon–Fri; Dinner: 5pm–midnight Mon, 5pm–1am Tue–Sat • KrKrKr*

8 Brasserie Elverket

The lunches are superb value and it serves unusual beers from the tap. *Linnégatan 69 • Map Q2 • 08 661 25 62 • Open Lunch: 11am–2pm Mon–Fri; Dinner: 5–10pm Mon–Wed; 5–11pm Thu–Sat • KrKr*

9 Restaurang Museet

A friendly bistro that serves good soups. *Birger Jarlsgatan 41 • Map M1 • 08 20 10 08 • Open 11am–11pm Mon–Tue, 11–1am Wed–Fri, 5pm–1am Sat, 5–11pm Sun • KrKrKr*

10 Grodan Grev Ture

A classic Swedish-European restaurant with an adjacent bar. *Grev Turegatan 16 • Map N2 • 08 679 61 00 • Open 11:30–12am Mon–Wed; 11:30–1am Thu–Fri, noon–1am Sat; 1–8pm Sun • KrKrKr*

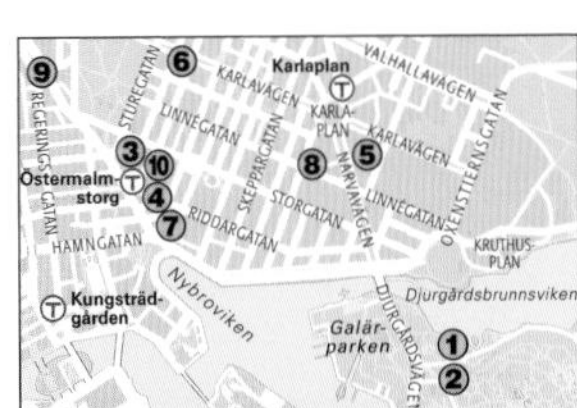

LA CANTINA

Left **Moderna Museet** Centre **Exhibits in Östasiatiska Museet** Right **Performers in Stortorget**

Gamla Stan, Skeppsholmen and Blasieholmen

THE SITE OF STOCKHOLM'S 13TH-CENTURY ORIGINS *and a well-preserved medieval city centre, Gamla Stan (Old Town) is one of Stockholm's most popular destinations. Away from tourist crowds, the narrow streets have a fairy-tale like feel, particularly at night and when the snow falls. The Royal Palace, one of the largest in the world, is the Old Town's major attraction, and there are also many beautiful churches, including Storkyrkan. Skeppsholmen is famous for its museums – Moderna Museet, with its collection of 20th-century art, and Östasiatiska Museet, housing Far Eastern antiquities, are two of them. The Grand Hotel dominates neighbouring Blasieholmen, also home to the Nationalmuseet.*

View of Gamla Stan with Skeppsholmsbron in front

TOP 10 Sights

1. **The Royal Palace**
2. **Storkyrkan**
3. **Stortorget**
4. **Christmas Market**
5. **Streets of Gamla Stan**
6. **Riddarholmen**
7. **Moderna Museet**
8. **Kastellholmen**
9. **Skeppsholmen Shoreline Walk**
10. **Nationalmuseet**

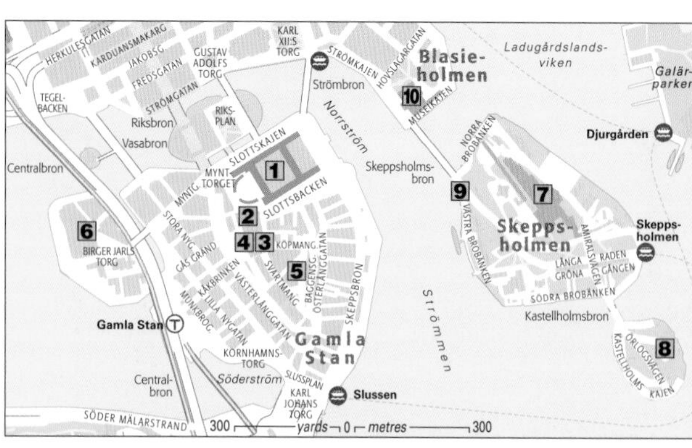

1 The Royal Palace

With more than 600 rooms, the Royal Palace, completed in 1754 in the Baroque style, is one of the biggest in Europe and still the venue for all state functions. It houses five museums, among them the Treasury, in the cellar vaults, with priceless state regalia such as crowns *(see pp20–21)*.

Sculpture in the Royal Palace

2 Storkyrkan

Stockholm's medieval cathedral, built in 1279, is of great religious importance. It is renowned for housing some extraordinary art treasures, including the *St George and the Dragon* sculpture (1489) carved from oak and elk horn. The legendary *Vädersoltavlan*, the "Sun Dog Painting", from 1636, is the oldest portrayal of the capital. Painted from high up on the cliffs of Södermalm, it shows the town as it was in the later Middle Ages. Since 1527, the cathedral has been a Lutheran church. A wide range of religious services and concerts are held there. *Trångsund 1 • Map M5*

Late Gothic interior of Storkyrkan

3 Stortorget

The city square, Stortorget, in the middle of Gamla Stan, is the oldest square in Stockholm and the site of the gruesome "Bloodbath" in 1520 *(see p32)*. Unlike many other European city squares, it was never developed as a showpiece: it slopes notably westwards and its buildings were constructed in a haphazard manner in the 17th and 18th centuries. The Stock Exchange Building (Börshuset), in French Rococo style, was completed in 1776 and houses the Nobelmuseet *(see p86)*. In a second hand shop on Stortorget 5, there are ceiling joists from the 1640s with pictures of animals, flowers and fruits. *Map M5*

4 Christmas Market

In winter, Stockholm takes on a magical atmosphere, and this is most evident in the traditional Christmas market in Storgorget. Little red huts sell home-made products – Christmas lights and decorations, handicrafts and clothes, festive sweets, smoked sausages, reindeer and elk meat and other delicacies from around Sweden.Get warm with a glass or two of "glögg" or mulled wine, and buy bottles of the unique Christmas drink, "julmust". *Stortorget • Map M5 • 24 Nov–23 Dec: 11am–6pm daily*

Crowded street in Gamla Stan

5 Streets of Gamla Stan

Västerlånggatan is the Old Town's main street; it is good for shopping but is also by far the most touristy street. At its southern end is Mårten Trotzigs Gränd, the city's narrowest street, with a width of just 90 cm (35 inches). More relaxed for strolling is Österlånggatan, home to several restaurants and unique shops, and the charming Köpmangatan, which leads directly to Stortorget. Stora Nygatan, close to the underground station, is a good street to unwind, with both Café Tabac and Wirströms Pub *(see p88)*. *Map M5*

6 Riddarholmen

The "Knight's Island" is cut off from Gamla Stan by a major road and a river, but is worth the diversion – it can be reached by a small bridge, Riddarhusbron. Usually tranquil, the island has some of the best views in Stockholm from Evert Taubes Terrass across the water to Lake Mälaren. Riddarholmen is home to Riddarholmskyrkan *(see p57)* and many 17th-century palaces, which now house offices. Walpurgis night *(see p39)* is celebrated here with a bonfire and singing. *Birger Jarls Torg • Map L5*

Preservation of Gamla Stan

The Old Town is one of Sweden's jewels – yet in the 1950s, when the modernization madness was at its peak, as part of the city's development plan, it was to be demolished. It was considered a slum and many of the buildings were decaying. Swedish author and journalist Vera Siöcrona led a successful campaign to save Gamla Stan from the bulldozers.

7 Moderna Museet

Set on the leafy island of Skeppsholmen, this fine modern art museum exhibits key works of 20th-century art, including those by Picasso, Salvador Dali, Henri Matisse, Giorgio De Chirico and many more. The collection includes some 5,000 paintings, sculptures and installations, as well as drawings, graphic works and photography. The museum also hosts first-class exhibitions of contemporary Swedish and international art. There is a children's workshop, a shop and a restaurant with a great view of Djurgården and Strandvägen *(see p35)*. *Map P5*

8 Kastellholmen

South of the Skeppsholmen is the tiny island of Kastellholmen, part of the national city park. Find a comfortable spot on its granite rocks and admire the small castle-like medieval building on the island. Cannons are fired here on the Swedish National

Royal tombs inside Riddarholmskyrkan

Day, 6 June, and on the birthdays of the King, Queen and Crown Princess. ⊗ *Map Q6*

9 Skeppsholmen Shoreline Walk

Skeppsholmen is ideal for a circular waterside walk any time of the year. Cross Skeppsholmsbron to the island, turn left and follow the path through a small doorway, and along the water to the quayside Östra Brobänken. Take in the smell of tar from the veteran boats moored here, and the fine views across the water. Catch a Djurgården ferry at the southeastern tip of the island, or continue in a circle past the af Chapman hostel *(see p115)*.
⊗ *Map P4*

Hostel af Chapman, Skeppsholmen

10 Nationalmuseet

This lavish museum houses Sweden's largest art collection, with some 16,000 classic paintings and sculptures. There is also a huge collection of drawings and engravings from the Renaissance to the present. The museum is currently under renovation – check its website for details. ⊗ *Map N4*
• *www.nationalmuseum.se*

A Day in Gamla Stan, Skeppsholmen and Blasieholmen

Morning

Start the day with a museum: Bus 65 from Stockholm's Central Station runs all the way to Skeppsholmen. Head for the **Moderna Museet** *(see p35)*, which opens at 10am every day except Monday. After a good morning's viewing of its fine 20th-century collection take a coffee break at **Café Bloms** *(see p88)* within the museum. Walk over Skeppsholmsbron and past the ferries to the **Nationalmuseet** and the **Grand Hotel** *(see p112)* before swinging back across Strömbron towards the **Royal Palace** *(see pp20–21)*. Walk up the cobbly Slottsbacken, and on to Gamla Stan's Österlånggatan. A good lunch stop is **Magnus Ladulås** *(see p89)*; enjoy a three-course meal in their traditional cellar restaurant.

Afternoon

Get purposefully lost along the narrow yet charming streets of Köpmangatan, aiming to end up at **Stortorget** *(see p83)*, the Old Town's main square. In good weather admire the square with a drink at **Chokladkoppen** *(see p88)*. The afternoon is one of the less busy times on Västerlånggatan; stroll south-eastwards and drop into the best of its shops. At the eastern end, do not miss the Old Town's narrowest street, Mårten Trotzigs Gränd. Round off the day with a drink and tapas with the locals, at popular **Café Tabac** *(see p88)*.

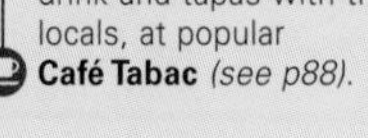

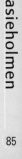

Left **Sculpture in Östasiatiska Museet** Centre **Arkitekturemuseet** Right **Interior of Tyska Kyrkan**

TOP 10 Best of the Rest

1 Arkitekturmuseet
Explore Swedish architecture from a thousand years ago to the present day. *Skeppsholmen • Map P5 • 08 587 270 70 • Open 10am–8pm Tue, 10am–6pm Wed–Sun • Adm • www.arkitekturmuseet.se*

2 Östasiatiska Museet
This museum houses superb collections from the Far East, India and Southeast Asia. *Skeppsholmen • Map P4 • 08 519 557 50 • Open noon–8pm Tue, noon–5pm Wed–Fri, 11am–5pm Sat & Sun • Adm • www.ostasiatiska.se*

3 Forum För Levande Historia
The Forum for Living History promotes tolerance, democracy and human rights. *Stora Nygatan 10 • Map M5 • 08 723 87 68 • Open noon–5pm Mon–Fri • www.levandehistoria.se*

4 Kungliga Myntkabinettet
The Royal Coin Cabinet has coins and notes, and examines the role of money. *Slottsbacken 6 • Map M5 • 08 519 553 04 • Open 10am–4pm daily • Adm • www.myntkabinettet.se*

5 Livrustkammaren
The Royal Armoury boasts an amazing collection of objects from Swedish royalty. *Slottsbacken 3 • Map M5 • 08 402 30 30 • Open 11am–5pm daily • Adm • www.livrustkammaren.se*

6 Nobelmuseet
Learn about the Nobel Prize and winners. The museum café serves the Nobel ice cream. *Stortorget • Map M5 • 08 534 818 00 • Open mid-May–mid-Sep: 10am–6pm daily (till 8pm Tue); mid-Sep–mid-May: 11am–8pm Tue, 11am–5pm Wed–Sun • Adm • www.nobelmuseum.se*

7 Postmuseum
This museum traces the history of the postal system from its origins to the present. *Lilla Nygatan 6 • Map M5 • 01 043 644 39 • Open 11am–4pm Tue–Sun; Sep–Apr: (till 7pm Wed) • Adm • www.postmuseum.posten.se*

8 Tyska Kyrkan
The German church was founded in 1571. *Svartmangatan 16 • Map M5 • 08 411 11 88 • Open 1 Oct–30 Apr: noon–4pm Wed, Fri & Sat, 12:30–4pm Sun; 1 May–30 Sep: noon–4pm daily*

9 Fotografins Hus
Contemporary photography is on display here. *Slupskjulsvägen 26c • Map P4 • 08 611 69 69 • Open noon–6pm Wed–Thu, noon–4pm Fri–Sun; closed summers • www.fotografinshus.se*

10 Story Tours
Discover the Old Town's charms on a walking tour. *Map M5 • 070 490 62 69 • Adm • www.storytours.eu*

Some museums have different opening hours for the summer and winter months.

Left **SF Bokhandeln** Centre **Women's clothing in Gudren Sjödén** Right **BluVelvet**

TOP 10 Places to Shop

1 Gudrun Sjödén

Colourful clothes for women with an emphasis on Scandinavian style. Designed by Gudrun Sjödén herself since the 1970s. *Stora Nygatan 33 • Map M5 • 08 23 55 55*

2 Iris Hantverk

Visually impaired craftsmen create function brushes at Iris Hantverk, which was established at the end of the 19th century. *Västerlånggatan 24 • Map M5 • 08 698 09 73*

3 Sweden Bookshop

Impressive selection of translated Swedish literature and books. There are over 2,000 titles in 47 languages. *Slottsbacken 10 • Map M5 • 08 453 78 00*

4 Kalikå

This store specializes in handmade soft toys, puppets and dolls – all made by mothers of Russian children with disabilities. Through a project called "Fair Play", mothers can stay home and care for their children and at the same time support themselves. This enables the children to stay at home rather than at a Russian orphanage. *Österlånggatan 18 • Map N5 • 08 20 52 19*

5 Indiska

A blend of fashion, interior design and accessories inspired by India, Indiska has a "bohemian modern" style. *Västerlånggatan 50 • Map M5 • 08 21 29 34*

6 Gustaf Mellbin

Established in 1867, this shop specializes in lingerie for big and small sizes. *Västerlånggatan 47 • Map M5 • 08 20 21 93*

7 SF Bokhandeln

A haven for science fiction fans, this store sells books, films, games and magazines. A large amount of its stock is in English. *Västerlånggatan 48 • Map M5 • 08 21 50 52*

8 BluVelvet

A huge selection of fun and trendy clothes, bags and accessories mainly for teens and women in their 20s is available here, though all lovers of funky items are welcome, regardless of age. *Västerlånggatan 32 • Map M5 • 08 10 58 28*

9 Kilgren

This store stocks high-quality traditional Scandinavian goods – especially classic clothing such as thick woolly sweaters, hats and socks. It also sells bracelets, Dala horses, knives and other homeware items. *Västerlånggatan 45 • Map M5 • 08 20 94 24*

10 Earth N More

This environmentally conscious store sells women's and men's clothes and accessories. Its motto it to only stock brands that "combine design, function and environment in an attractive way". *Stora Nygatan 14 • Map M5 • 08 641 02 10*

Not all stores are open on Sundays.

Left **Cadierbar's contemporary decor** Right **Signage outside Wirströms Pub**

TOP 10 Cafés, Pubs and Bars

1 Café Tabac

Tapas bar that serves coffee, snacks or a full meal. *Stora Nygatan 46 • Map M5 • 08 10 15 34 • Open 10am–midnight Mon–Thu, 10–1am Fri–Sat, 11am–midnight Sun*

2 Wirströms Pub

This popular pub attracts a mix of students, tourists and locals. *Stora Nygatan 13 • Map M5 • 08 21 28 74 • Open Mon–Sat 11–1am, noon–1am Sun*

3 Stampen

Founded in 1968, this long-standing jazz and blues bar has live music every night. *Stora Nygatan 5 • Map M5 • 08 20 57 93 • Open 5pm–1am Mon–Thu, 5pm–2am Fri–Sat, 1–5pm on some Sun*

4 Lydmar Hotel Bar

Great drinks are served in this stylish bar located in the Lydmar Hotel. *Södra Blasieholmshamnen 2 • Map N4 • 08 22 31 60 • Open 11am–midnight Mon–Sun (till 1am Fri & Sat) • www.lydmar.com*

5 Café Bloms in Moderna Museet

This café serves light snacks, drinks and pastries. It also has a covered outdoor area in the museum's Picasso Park. *Skeppsholmen 7 • Map P4 • 08 519 562 91 • Open 11am–5:30pm Tue–Sun*

6 Monks Porter House

Sister pub to Monks Café and Brewery *(see p66)*, Monks Porter House has 56 different beers on tap. It also brews darker ales and stouts. *Munkbron 11 • Map M5 • 08 23 12 12 • Open from 5pm Tue–Thu, from 4pm Fri & Sat; closes at 1am or earlier if not busy; closed 22 Jun–14 Aug*

7 Pubologi

A sleek yet cosy gastropub, Pubologi has an imaginative menu which handpicks pub and bar-style food from across Europe. *Stora Nygatan 20 • Map M5 • 08 506 400 86 • Open 6:30–11pm Mon–Sat; closed summer • www.pubologi.se*

8 Cadierbar, Grand Hotel

Enjoy a glass of quality wine or a cocktail at this elegant bar located within the Grand Hotel. *Södra Blaiseholmshamnen 8 • Map N4 • 08 679 35 00 • Open 7–2am Mon–Fri, 8–2am Sat, 8–1am Sun*

9 Ardbeg Embassy

This specialist whiskey bar also has a wide selection of beers from Swedish microbreweries. It serves high-quality, pricey food. *Västerlånggatan 68 • Map M5 • 08 791 90 90 • Open 4–11pm Mon–Tue, 4pm–midnight Wed–Thu, 11–1am Fri, noon–1am Sat, 4–10pm Sun*

10 Chokladkoppen

A gay-friendly café in the Old Town's main square; good for information about upcoming gay events in the city. *Stortorget 18 • Map M5 • 08 20 31 70 • Summer: open 9am–11pm daily; Winter: open 10am–10pm Mon–Thu, 10am–11pm Fri; 9am–11pm Sat, 9am–10pm Sun*

It is usually cheaper to buy a bottle of wine rather than ordering several individual glasses.

Price Categories

For a three-course meal for one with half a bottle of wine (or equivalent meal), taxes and extra charges.

Ⓚ	400–550 kr
ⓀⓀ	550–700 kr
ⓀⓀⓀ	700–1000 kr
ⓀⓀⓀⓀ	over 1000 kr

Left **Pizza at Vapiano Gamla Stan** Right **Lobsters and crabs at B.A.R.**

TOP 10 Places to Eat

1 Brasserie Le Rouge

Classy but cool French-themed restaurant with opulent interiors. *Brunnsgränd 2 • Map N5 • 08 505 244 30 • Open 6pm–1am Tue, 5pm–1am Wed–Sun; closed summers •* ⓀⓀⓀ

2 Hotell Skeppsholmen Restaurant

Modern Swedish cuisine is served at this stylishly simple hotel's *(see p116)* restaurant. *Gröna Gången 1 • Map P5 • 08 407 23 05 • Open 11:30am–10pm Mon–Fri, noon–10pm Sat, noon–9pm Sun •* ⓀⓀⓀ

3 Mathias Dahlgren

Food in this restaurant in the Grand Hotel is prepared by one of Sweden's top chefs. *Sodra Blaiseholmshamnen 6 • Map N4 • 08 679 35 00 • Open 7pm–midnight Tue–Sat • www.grandhotel.se •* ⓀⓀⓀ

4 B.A.R.

Excellent seafood restaurant; pick from grilled fish of the day. *Blasieholmsgatan 4a • Map N3 • 08 611 53 35 • Open 10–1am Mon–Fri, 4pm–1am Sat, 5–9pm Sun •* ⓀⓀⓀ

5 Restaurang JT

This traditional Swedish place offers a reliable choice. *Järntorget 78 • Map M6 • 08 20 44 20 • Open 11am–midnight Mon–Fri, noon–midnight Sat & Sun •* ⓀⓀⓀ

6 Den Gyldene Freden

Old-fashioned, classic restaurant that opened in 1722. *Österlånggatan 51 • Map N5 • 08 24 97 60 • Open 11:30am–2:30pm & 5–10pm Mon–Thu, 11:30am–2:30pm & 5pm–11pm Fri, 1–11pm Sat •* ⓀⓀⓀ

7 Magnus Ladulås

The three-course meal offers in this cosy cellar restaurant in the Old Town are particularly good. *Österlånggatan 26 • Map N5 • 08 21 19 57 • Lunch: Open 11am–2pm Mon–Fri; Dinner: Open 11am–11pm Mon–Tue; till midnight Wed & Thu, till 1am Fri–Sat •* ⓀⓀ

8 Vapiano Gamla Stan

Worldwide chain with the motto "fast, fresh and casual", Vapiano serves decent pasta and pizza. *Munkbrogatan 8 • Map M5 • 08 22 29 40 • Open 11am–midnight Sun–Thu; 11am–1am Fri–Sat •* Ⓚ

9 Frantzen/Lindeberg

Have a gourmet experience in this Michelin-starred place that picks vegetables from its gardens. *Lilla Nygatan 21 • Map M5 • 08 20 85 80 • Open 6pm–1am Tue–Sat •* ⓀⓀⓀⓀ

10 Bistro Pastis

Authentic French bistro with a homely feel. *Baggensgatan 12 • Map M5 • 08 20 20 18 • Lunch: Open Mon-Fri; Dinner: Mon-Sat •* ⓀⓀⓀ

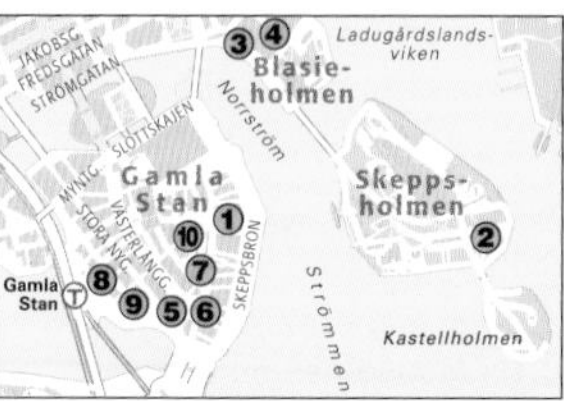

Although some restaurants are open until late the kitchen may close earlier.

Left **Fotografiska Museet shop** Right **Monteliusvägen's viewing platform**

Södermalm

FORMERLY A ROUGH WORKING-CLASS DISTRICT OF THE CITY, *Södermalm has been transformed over the last couple of decades, blossoming into the area to see and be seen in. "Söder" offers a blend of affordable neighbourhood restaurants, cool cafés, trendy shopping and a vibrant nightlife. The area has lots of greenery, and as it is hilly, some of the best views over Stockholm – particularly from Monteliusvägen, looking across Lake Mälaren to Stadshuset. There is no shortage of museums either – notably the Fotografiska Museet, which has earned immense international acclaim. For a lively side to the city, Söder is the place to be.*

Gondolen restaurant in Södermalm

A park in Nytorget square

Top 10 Sights

1. Tantolunden
2. Medborgarplatsen
3. Skånegatan
4. Spårvägsmuseet
5. Fotografiska Museet
6. Mosebacke and Mosebacke Torg
7. Mariatorget
8. Stockholms Stadsmuseum
9. Monteliusvägen
10. Långholmen

Allotment cottage in Tantolunden

1 Tantolunden

People meet for swimming and picnics in this large park by the waters of Årstaviken bay in summer – it can get a bit overrun on sunny weekends – and for sledding in winter. There is a playground, beach volleyball court and golf, plus cafés. The park is sometimes used as a festival area, notably for the annual Stockholm Pride festival *(see p38)*. Move away from the crowds and wander up the hill amidst more than 100 lovingly maintained allotment gardens and cottages. The Zinkensdamm hotel and hostel *(see p114)* is located in the park. *Map B6*

2 Medborgarplatsen

"Civic Square" lives up to its name with a host of communal activities in and around it. In summer it comes alive with a row of outdoor bars and restaurants; in winter there is an ice-skating rink in the centre. It is bordered by the Debaser Medis *(see p50)* nightclub and bar – the club takes its name "medis" from the square and baths here – and the Saluhall shopping and entertainment centre, including bars, good restaurants and a cinema.

Map D5

3 Skånegatan

The focal point of SoFo *(see p40)*, Skånegatan is one of the city's most "happening" streets with designer shops and alternative bars such as Snotty Sounds Bar and Pet Sounds Bar *(see p94)*. Families descend on the area around Nytorget square during the day, and it is not far to Vitabergsparken, which stages events for open-air music and dance in summer. Bars and restaurants in the area are lively at night, even on weekdays.

Map D6

4 Spårvägsmuseet

While this transport museum begins with the horse and cart and simple ferry boats, the main focus is the expansion of the public transport network in the 20th century. Visitors climb aboard trams and buses to be whisked back in time: films projected through tram windows re-create travelling in Stockholm in the 1950s and 1960s. A former tram stop kiosk has been faithfully reproduced and children can ride aboard a mini-train.

Tegelsviksgatan 22 • Map F6 • 08 686 17 60 • Open 10am–5pm Mon–Fri, 11am–4pm Sat–Sun • Adm • www.sparvagsmuseet.sl.se

Vintage bus at Spårvägsmuseet

The outdoor bars and restaurants at Medborgarplatsen are open from around April until September.

Summer crowds at the popular Mariatorget

5 Fotografiska Museet

Billed as a centre for contemporary photography, Fotografiska Museet was opened in 2010 to host works by famous photographers. The brick building from 1906 at the waterfront that houses it was formerly a customs house – it now includes a bistro, café and bar.

Stadsgårdshamnen 22 • Map E5 • 08 509 005 00 • www.fotografiska.eu

6 Mosebacke and Mosebacke Torg

The district of Mosebacke has become a cultural centre thanks to Södra Teatern (theatre) and its bar *(see p49)*. When the weather turns milder, the large open-air section of Södra Bar is crowded every evening. Mosebacke Torg, the square, is much more peaceful – an oasis with a small summer café selling tasty cinnamon buns. *Map D5*

Stieg Larsson's Stockholm

Södermalm has become famous with the popularity of Stieg Larsson's Millennium trilogy – particularly since the Hollywood version of *The Girl With the Dragon Tattoo* was partly filmed on Söder. Pick up a "Millennium Map" from the tourist information office – tour locations include Mellqvist's Kaffebar, where Larsson himself used to hang out.

7 Mariatorget

One of the prettiest city squares, Mariatorget is a popular meeting place year round and attracts plenty of sunbathers in summer. It is the perfect spot to rest tired feet when exploring Södermalm. Mariatorget is also the venue for the 10-day long Maria Boule competitions and festival *(see p55)*. There is a host of cafés and restaurants nearby. St Paulskyrkan, a small Methodist church, faces the southwest corner of the square. *Map C5*

8 Stockholms Stadsmuseum

Stockholms Stadsmuseum is dedicated to the urban history of the city and illustrates the daily life of Stockholmers. The "City Square" is a delight for children – they can load carts and carry sacks, wrap fish up in newspaper and play at market stalls. A kiosk from the 1970s sells sweets by weight. *Ryssgården • Map D5 • 08 508 316 00 • Open 11am–5pm Tue, Wed, Fri, Sat & Sun, 11am–8pm Thu • Adm • www.stadsmuseum.stockholm.se*

9 Monteliusvägen

This 500-m (1640-ft) long walking path adjacent to the popular Ivar Los Park offers magnificent views of Lake Mälaren, Stadshuset, Old Town

Bus 4 connects many parts of Södermalm, from Skanstull to Hornstull.

and Riddarholmen, especially at sunrise and sunset. Constructed in 1998 on a precipice, it has charming old houses on one side and wonderful views on the other as well as benches and picnic tables to enjoy them from. However, the path has areas of clay and wooden planks that can be very slippery in winter. On Blecktomsgränd, leading down to Mariatorget towards the eastern end of the walk, there are several cosy cafés. *Map L6*

Långholmen boat park

10 Långholmen

This hilly island is a locals' favourite for walking, picnics, swimming and recreation. Yet from 1880 to 1975, it was home to the country's biggest prison, and Sweden's last execution took place here in 1910. The prison has been converted into a hotel and youth hostel *(see p116)*. The island has beaches and open-air stages, and is also home to Mälarvarvet, one of Stockholm's oldest shipyards. There is a fine view towards Stadshuset and Gamla Stan from its eastern shores. *Map A4*

A day in Södermalm

Morning

Start the day with coffee or breakfast at **Mellqvist Kaffebar** *(see p94)* then take the short walk up Torkel Knutsonssgatan to the scenic walk along **Monteliusvägen** towards Slussen. After enjoying the views across Lake Mälaren, descend to Hornsgatan and pop into **Maria Magdalena Kyrka** *(see p57)* and **Stockholms Stadsmuseum**. Rising like a crane over Slussen is an old "lift", on top of which is Gondolen *(see p95)*, which is quite a unique place to eat. Its menu offers by far its best value at lunchtime.

Afternoon

From Gondolen it is just a short walk to the picturesque square at **Mosebacke**; if the weather is good, this a lovely place to relax and digest your lunch. Walk around the square till you reach Östgötagatan; follow it down the hill, perhaps taking a short diversion to **Katarina Kyrka** *(see p56)* and its attractive grounds. Cross Folkungagatan and reach the heart of **SoFo** *(see p40)*. After browsing the design shops in the area, walk southeast along Bondegatan to the **Spårvägsmuseet** *(see p91)* and the **Leksaksmuseet** *(see p37)* housed in the same building; late afternoon is often not so busy and a good time to visit these places. Return to Skånegatan for dinner at **Nytorget Urban Deli** *(see p42)* and maybe even an after-dinner drink at **Snotty Sounds Bar** or **Pet Sounds Bar** *(see p94)*.

Alight at Medborgarplatsen underground station for SoFo.

Left **Table setting at Strand** Centre **Tray of drinks at Mellqvist Kaffebar** Right **Oliver Twist**

TOP 10 Cafés, Pubs and Bars

1 Marie Laveau
Cajun-style restaurant with a club below that opens at night. *Hornsgatan 66 • Map C5 • 08 668 85 00 • www.marielaveau.se*

2 Morfar Ginko and Pappa Ray Ray
Sit outside on the street front or in the cosy courtyard in summer. It serves both bar snacks and full meals. *Swedenborgsgatan 13 • Map C5 • 08 641 13 40*

3 Strand
A good place to relax at the bar. In winters, it opens for brunch from 11am on weekends. *Hornstulls Strand 4 • Map A5 • 08 658 63 50 • Open 5pm–midnight Tue, 5pm–2am Wed & Thu, 5pm–3am Fri & Sat • www.hornstullstrand.se*

4 Kvarnen
An old-fashioned beer hall, Kvarnen becomes a nightclub on weekends. *Tjärhovsgatan 4 • Map D5 • 08 643 03 80 • Open 11–3am Mon–Sat, noon–11pm Sat & Sun*

5 Söders Hjärta
Visit this friendly place for an early evening snack, to play pinball or relax at the bar. *Bellmansgatan 22b • Map C5 • 08 640 14 62*

6 Mellqvist Kaffebar
Renowned for its coffee, Mellqvist Kaffebar also has good breakfast deals. *Hornsgatan 78 • Map C5 • 07 687 529 92 • Open 7am–6pm Mon–Fri, 9am–6pm Sat & Sun*

7 Babylon
Hidden in a park just across the road from bustling Medborgarplatsen, Babylon's long, narrow bar is perfect for almost any time of the day or year. *Björns Trädgårdsgränd • Map D5 • 08 640 80 83 • Open 11am–midnight daily*

8 Pet Sounds Bar
Named after the Beach Boys' "Pet Sounds" album and the record store across the road of the same name, this place takes its music seriously. DJs play both in the upstairs bar and in the cellar at weekends. It has a good selection of beers. *Skånegatan 80 • Map D6 • 08 643 82 25 • Open 5pm–midnight Tue, 5pm–1am Wed–Sat*

9 Snotty Sounds Bar
Probably the only "hole in the wall" music bar in the city, Snotty has pictures of new wave and punk icons on the walls and tunes to match. It is small and can get extremely crowded at weekends. *Skånegatan 90 • Map D6 • 08 644 39 10 • Open 4pm–1am daily*

10 Oliver Twist
One of the very few pubs in Sweden serving cask-conditioned ale, this is just the right place for beer connoisseurs to meet. It is lively most nights, with a friendly crowd. *Repslagargatan 6 • Map D5 • 08 640 05 66 • Open 11am–11pm Mon; 11–1am Tue–Fri, noon–1am Sat; noon–11pm Sun*

Some bars do not accept credit cards or may charge for small transactions such as those under 100 kr.

Left **Nytorget Urban Deli's outdoor seating**

Price Categories

For a three-course meal for one with half a bottle of wine (or equivalent meal), taxes and extra charges.

Ⓚ	400–550 kr
ⓀⓀ	550–700 kr
ⓀⓀⓀ	700–1000 kr
ⓀⓀⓀⓀ	over 1000 kr

Top 10 Places to Eat

1 Nostrano

This Italian neighbourhood place is great for an intimate dinner. *Timmermansgatan 13 • Map C5 • 08 644 10 35 • Open 5pm–midnight Mon–Sat • www.nostrano.se • ⓀⓀ*

2 Dado

An Indian restaurant with an adventurous menu that is a cut above the rest in the area. *Tavasgatan 28 • Map C5 • 08 669 92 20 • Open 5:30pm–11pm Tue–Thu, 5–11pm Fri–Sun • ⓀⓀ*

3 Gondolen

Atop Katarinahissen, a Stockholm landmark, it has great views. The lunch menu is the value option. *Stadsgården 6 • Map D5 • 08 641 70 90 • Lunch: Open 11:30am–2:30pm Mon–Fri; Dinner: Open 5pm–1am Mon–Fri, 4pm–1am Sat • ⓀⓀⓀⓀ*

4 Sardin

This tiny 18-seater restaurant serves small tapas dishes. *Skånegatan 79 • Map E6 • 08 644 97 00 Open 5pm–midnight Mon–Sat • ⓀⓀ*

5 Nytorget Urban Deli

A restaurant, bar and food store with a lively New York feel specializing in shellfish and grilled meats. *Nytorget 4 • Map E6 • 08 599 091 80 • Open 8am–11pm Sun–Tue, 8am–midnight Wed–Thu 8–1am Fri–Sat • ⓀⓀ*

6 Pelikan

Eat traditional Swedish food in a historical setting. *Blekingegatan 40 • Map D6 • 08 556 090 90 • Open 4pm–midnight Mon–Thu 1pm–1am Fri & Sat; 1–11pm Sun • www.pelikan.se • ⓀⓀ*

7 Faros

This family-run restaurant serves Greek food in hearty portions. *Sofiagatan 1 • Map E6 • 08 641 23 64 • Open 4pm–midnight Mon–Fri, 1pm–midnight Sat, noon–11pm Sun • ⓀⓀ*

8 Hjördis

A homely, neighbourhood restaurant, Hjördis has a mostly Mediterranean-based menu. *Borgmästargatan 7 • Map E5 • 08 640 99 50 • Open 11am–11pm Tue, 11am–midnight Wed–Thu, 11–1am Fri, 5pm–1am Sat, 5–10pm Sun • ⓀⓀⓀ*

9 Blå Dörren

"The blue door" serves traditional Swedish food. *Södermalmstorg 6 • Map D5 • 08 743 07 43 • Open 10:30am–11pm Mon, 10:30am–midnight Tue–Thu, 10:30–1am Fri, 1pm–1am Sat, 1–11pm Sun • ⓀⓀ*

10 Hermans

Variety in vegetarian food is Hermans' mission. *Fjällgatan 23B • Map E5 • 08 643 94 80 • Open 11am–9pm daily • Ⓚ*

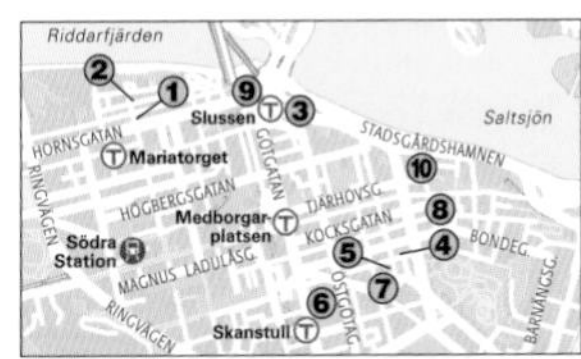

Many restaurants are very popular right from opening time and advance booking is recommended.

Left **Stora Pelousen in Hagaparken** Right **Glass gondolas on tracks on Globen's exterior**

Further Afield

IT IS EASY TO SPREAD YOUR WINGS BEYOND STOCKHOLM – *and there are sights aplenty. SL period travel cards make for exceptional value if you want to roam – the Greater Stockholm travel card zone extends right down to the port of Nynäshamn in the south and beyond Norrtälje in the north. Buses usually run to the most out-of-the-way sights; even the vast wilderness of Tyresö National Park is accessible by public transport. The beautiful city of Uppsala is one of the best day trips from Stockholm, with fast, frequent direct trains. To the east, the Stockholm Archipelago is a holiday destination in itself with around 30,000 islands to explore.*

Boats in the Stockholm Archipelago

TOP 10 Sights

1. **Uppsala**
2. **Sigtuna**
3. **Birka**
4. **Mariefred**
5. **Drottningholm**
6. **Hagaparken**
7. **Globen**
8. **Naturhistoriska Riksmuseet**
9. **Millesgården**
10. **Stockholm Archipelago**

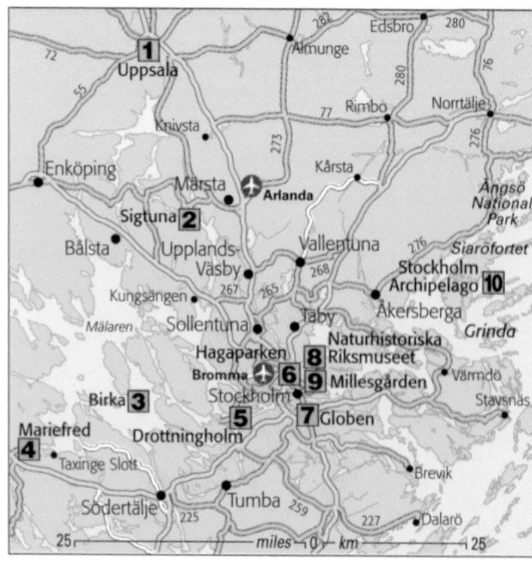

Storstockholms Lokaltrafik (SL) travelcards are available for 24 or 72 hours, 7 days, 30 days or 90 days.

Shaded path with benches along the riverside, Uppsala

1 Uppsala

Sweden's fourth biggest city and a major university town founded in 1164, Uppsala is picturesque and lively, with a striking cathedral. Regular trains take under an hour from Stockholm to Uppsala station, right in the city centre.

2 Sigtuna

Founded in 980, Sigtuna is Sweden's oldest city. It has a very popular centre, with low wooden houses, lots of cafés, craft shops and a charming museum. There are ruins of two churches – St Olof's and St Per's. The city can be easily reached by local train to Märsta followed by a short connecting bus ride. Boat trips also operate from Stockholm in summer, travelling through Lake Mälaren.

3 Birka

A UNESCO World Heritage Site, Birka is one of the most complete examples of a Viking trading settlement from around the 8th–9th century. While practically nothing remains above ground of the Birka that existed during that era, a museum illustrates how the town looked and functioned and there are some remarkable finds here. The island itself is calm and unspoilt with sheep and bull calves roaming about. Birka can be reached by boat trips in the summer.

4 Mariefred

Dominated by the fairytale-like Gripsholm Castle, the charming town of Mariefred is characterized by narrow streets and low wooden buildings in soft colours, mostly dating from the 18th and 19th centuries. It is a popular day trip; in summer take the steamboat, *S/S Mariefred*, from Stadshuskajen, next to Stadshuset, which leaves at 10am and returns from Mariefred at 4:30pm. It is also possible to take a train from Stockholm to Läggesta and change to the narrow-gauge Östra Södermalms steam railway to Mariefred (spring–autumn only). Combine the trip with a visit to Taxinge Slott *(see p100)*.

Gripsholm Castle in Mariefred

Drottningholm Palace and Gardens

5 Drottningholm

One of the best day trips from Stockholm, Drottningholm's Royal Palace and its park is one of three UNESCO World Heritage sites in and around the city. The palace, dating from the 17th century, is superbly preserved and is the official residence of the royal family. The park, combining styles from the formal to the wild and romantic, is worth a visit in itself *(see pp18–19)*.

6 Hagaparken

This "English Park" has softly shaped lawns interspersed with dark forests where paths meander amidst elegant trees, and with pavillions and ruins offering constant surprises. It lies just north of the city's boundary and is very easily reached by bus *(see pp28–9)*.

7 Globen

Officially named the Ericsson Globe, not only is Globen an excellent indoor arena for sport and concerts, but is the largest hemispherical building in the world. The white ball can be seen for miles around – and since 2010, it is possible to travel to the top to enjoy great views through a glass gondola running on tracks built on the globe's exterior. The trip is popular – even weddings take place in the gondolas – so book ahead. *Globentorget 2 • 07 718 110 00 • Open 9am–7pm Mon–Fri; 9:30am–6pm Sat–Sun; extended opening hours in summer • Adm: Skyview • www.globearenas.se*

8 Naturhistoriska Riksmuseet

The natural sciences are presented in a lively and interactive manner at this natural history museum. Exhibits showcase everything from the history of life and the origin of species to visits to polar regions and the treasures of the earth's interior. Adventures with dinosaurs and in outer space come to life at the IMAX cinema, Cosmonova. *Frescativägen 40 • Map D1 • 08 519 540 40 • www.nrm se*

Exhibit in Naturhistoriska Riksmuseet

9 Millesgården

This spectacular park overlooking the water includes sculptor Carl Milles's most famous works arranged on terraces below his former home. In 1936, Carl and his wife Olga donated Millesgården to the Swedes; castings of some of his sculptures are still sold in very limited editions to help fund its upkeep. Millesgården

Stockholm public transport runs 365 days a year, with a slightly reduced service on Midsummer, Christmas and New Year's Day.

is an easy and pleasant trip from Stockholm; take the tram from Ropsten.

Herserudsvägen 32, Lidingö
• *www.millesgarden.se*

Sculptures in Millesgården

Carl Milles

Carl Milles (1875–1955) is Sweden's most famous sculptor. He was an assistant to Auguste Rodin in Paris and spent over 20 years in the United States – many major municipal buildings in America include his sculptures. Milles and his wife Olga acquired the house at Millesgården in 1906, and its spacious terraces were developed over the next 50 years.

10 Stockholm Archipelago

One could spend weeks exploring Stockholm's peerless archipelago, but on a short trip there is always time to sample its delights, even without taking a boat. An hour by bus will take the visitor to a seaside spot such as Björkvik; otherwise it is just a 25-minute boat ride to Fjäderholmarna – the archipelago village at Stockholm's doorstep. The most luxurious choice, however, is to depart on one of the classic white steamboats, some of which date from the 19th century *(see pp12–13)*.

Day trip to Uppsala

Morning

Uppsala *(see p97)* is perfect for a day trip, with most of its sights concentrated in the historic western side of the city. The town centre is within easy walking distance from the central railway station. On arrival, turn right out of the station; it is a short walk to the north to the beautifully laid-out Linnaeus Garden and Museum and Botanical Gardens. Cross the river and swing back along its course to the **Uppsala Cathedral** dating back to the 13th century and the tallest church building in Scandinavia. King Gustav Vasa is buried here. **Hambergs Fisk** *(see p101)* is just a stone's throw from the cathedral, and as one of the best-rated restaurants in the city, an ideal stop for lunch. Its lunch menu offers excellent value compared to the evening à la carte dishes.

Afternoon

On the eastern side of Uppsala station is the terminus of the **Lennakatten narrow gauge railway** *(see p100)*. The 32-km (20-mile) route wends through forests and past lakes, with six different station stops: for a return trip to Marielund allow around two hours, which will allow ample time for a stroll and refreshments in the station café. From Uppsala there are regular trains for Stockholm: around three direct trains per hour until late evening. If staying in for dinner, the last direct train to Stockholm from Uppsala departs around 10pm.

Check out the website **http://sl.se/en/Visitor/Plan-your-journey/** *when planning a local trip.*

Left **Torekällberget Museum** Centre **Tom Tits Experiment** Right **Way to Östra station**

Top 10 Best of the Rest

1 Tyresta National Park
Just 20 km (12 miles) from central Stockholm, this national park is a vast area of unspoilt beauty, superb for hiking. *Tyresta village, 136 59 Vendelsö • 08 745 33 94 • Bus 807 & 809*

2 Torekällberget Outdoor Museum, Södertälje
The museum houses a village, exhibitions and several animals that were once common on farms in the area. *Torekällberget, 151 89 Södertälje • 08 523 014 22 • Open 1 Sep–31 May: 10am–4pm daily; 1 Jun–31 Aug: 10am–6pm daily*

3 Björnö
Located on the archipelago island Ingarö, Björnö nature reserve has beaches and secluded spots for sunbathing. Camping facilities are availiable. *Map H2 • Bus 428 & 429*

4 Skogskyrkogården
Greta Garbo is buried in this cemetery, a UNESCO World Heritage Site. Guided tours are available. *Skogskyrkogården • 08 508 317 30*

5 Saltsjöbaden
Take the Saltsjöbanen light train to this beautiful seaside resort. An organic café, Stationhuset, sells lunches and snacks year round.

6 Steninge Slott
This Baroque palace is located by the waters of Lake Mälaren near Märsta. It hosts a Christmas market and has shops selling Swedish crafts. *Steninge Slottsväg 141, 195 91 Märsta • Train from Stockholm to Märsta, then Bus 580 and walk 2 km(1 mile). • 08 592 595 00 • Currently closed for renovation*

7 Tom Tits Experiment, Södertälje
Spend at least half a day in this interactive science museum with attractions for all ages. *Storgatan 33, 151 36 Södertälje • 08 550 225 00 • Open 10am–4pm Tue–Fri, 11am–5pm Sat–Sun • Adm*

8 Lennakatten narrow gauge railway, Uppsala
Board this narrow-gauge steam train from Uppsala through dense forests and lakes. *Uppsala Östra station, Uppsala • 01 813 05 00 • Open from early Jun–early-Sep • Adm*

9 Taxinge Slott
This castle is famous for its cake buffet featuring around 60 types of locally baked cakes. See website for open hours. *Taxinge Slott, Taxinge • 01 597 01 14 • www.taxingeslott.se*

10 Västerås
One of Sweden's oldest cities, Västerås has many museums, a cathedral, botanic garden and is good for shopping.

Table setting at Mistral

Price Categories

For a three-course meal for one, with half a bottle of wine (or equivalent meal), taxes and extra charges.

Ⓚ	400–550 kr
ⓀⓀ	550–700 kr
ⓀⓀⓀ	700–1000 kr
ⓀⓀⓀⓀ	over 1000 kr

Top 10 Cafés and Restaurants

1 Mistral

This organic gourmet restaurant serves classy food. *Sockenvägen 529, Enskede • 08 10 12 24 • Open from 6pm Tue–Sat •* ⓀⓀⓀⓀ

2 Landet

Landet has almost single-handedly made the area around Telefonplan trendy; it is a restaurant, bar, club and live music venue rolled into one. *LM Ericssons väg 27, Telefonplan • 08 410 193 20 • Open 5pm–midnight Mon–Thu, 5pm–1am Fri–Sat •* ⓀⓀ

3 Sjöpaviljongen

Set in beautiful waterside surroundings by Essinge bay, Sjöpaviljongen has a lovely terrace to eat on in summer evenings. *Traneberg Strand 4, Bromma • 08 704 04 24 • Open 11:15am–10pm Mon–Fri, noon–10pm Sat, noon–9pm Sun •* ⓀⓀ

4 Båthuset

This floating restaurant exudes quality and has a homely ambience. Art exhibitions with paintings for sale adorn the walls. *Hamnen, Sigtuna • 08 592 567 80 • Open May–Sep: 6–10pm Tue–Sat; Oct–Apr: 6–9pm Wed–Sat •* ⓀⓀⓀ

5 Gåshaga Sealodge Restaurant

Relax in this restaurant with great views over the archipelago. *Värdhusvägen 14–16, Lidingö • 08 601 34 00 • Open noon–2:30pm & 4:30–9pm Mon–Sat, noon–4pm Sun •* ⓀⓀ

6 Fjärderholmarnas Rökeriet

An idyllic archipelago dining experience, the Rökeriet specializes in seafood. *Fjärderholmarna • 08 716 50 88 • Open May–Sep: noon–10pm daily •* ⓀⓀⓀ

7 Stationshuset, Saltsjöbaden

Organic food is served in this former station house where trains from Slussen to the resort of Saltsjöbaden terminate. It is very handy for a snack or light meal. *Saltsjöbaden station • 08 556 266 00 • Open 9am–5pm Mon–Fri, 10am–5pm Sat–Sun; Bistro: 7pm–10pm Fri •* ⓀⓀ

8 Skärgårdskrogen i Saltsjöbaden

This is a true archipelago dining experience just a short trip by train from Slussen. Open for lunch year round. *Vikingavägen 17a, Saltsjöbaden • 08 717 15 60 • Open Sep–Apr: 10:30am–2pm Mon–Fri; May–Aug: 10:30am–late daily •* ⓀⓀ

9 Bistro Edsbacka, Sollentuna

Luxury eating in a laid-back atmosphere; the menu is classic Swedish with a French twist. *Sollentunavägen 223 • 08 631 00 34 • Open 11:30am–11pm Tue–Fri, 4–11pm Sat •* ⓀⓀⓀ

10 Hambergs Fisk

Seafood restaurant with a French bistro-like atmosphere. *Fyristorg 8, Uppsala • 01 871 21 50 • Open 11:30am–10pm Tue–Sat •* ⓀⓀⓀ

Summer-only restaurants are usually open from early May to mid-September.

70 52

STREETSMART

Left **Tourist with luggage** Centre **Autumn colours** Right **Cosy bedroom in a hotel**

TOP 10 Planning Your Trip

1 When to Go

May through August sees the city in full bloom and it is never over-crowded – in high summer you may have some areas almost to yourself as the locals head for the countryside. During major events, such as the Stockholm Marathon in June, availability of hotels is scarce, so book well in advance. September is great, with blue skies and pretty foliage. December to February is also a delightful time to visit when some of the most important events are staged during the run-up to Christmas.

2 Climate

Stockholm is a city of climatic contrasts. Summer can be unusually warm – hot even – with restaurants spilling out on to the streets. Spring and autumn are both quite brief. Wrap up for winter – the temperature can drop as low as –20° C (–4° F) and it rarely rises above zero between November and March.

3 What to Pack

In summer, light clothing and rain wear will suffice, but bring a jacket for chillier evenings; sometimes even days. In winter, warm clothes are a must from November to early April – lots of layers, boots, coats, gloves and a hat. Dress code is mainly casual except for the most formal occasions.

4 Passports and Visas

Citizens of the European Union (EU) and European Economic Area (EEA) may enter Sweden and stay for as long as they please, though they should register with the local authorities after 90 days. Citizens of the USA, Canada and Australia can enter and stay visa-free for 90 days. Citizens of other countries are advised to check their visa requirements with their local Swedish embassy or consulate before travelling.

5 Currency

Sweden's currency is the Swedish krona (SEK or kr, plural kronor), though the euro may be accepted in a few establishments. All major credit cards are accepted even for the smallest transactions, though some bars have reverted to a cash only policy. Automatic cash machines (ATMs) are widely available throughout the city.

6 Time Zone

Stockholm is in the Central European Time (CET) zone, one hour ahead of Greenwich Mean Time (GMT) and six hours ahead of US Standard Time. Swedish summer time begins on the last Sunday in March and ends on the last Sunday in October, in line with the rest of Europe.

7 Customs

There are no customs restrictions for EU citizens if goods are for personal use. Arrivals from outside the EU can import a litre of spirits or four litres of wine, or 16 litres of beer. You can also bring 200 cigarettes, or 50 cigars, or 250 grams of loose tobacco.

8 Choosing a Hotel

Hotels in Stockholm do not come cheap, but the upside is that you can expect good standards of accommodation. With a fast and frequent public transport system running through the city, budget travellers can consider some of the low-price hotels located outside the city centre.

9 How Long to Stay

Most of Stockholm's major attractions are in a relatively compact area, so the city definitely works for a long weekend trip. But to get the best out of your visit, including some of the major museums, shopping and a boat trip to the archipelago, plan at least a week's stay.

10 Electricity

Electricity is 220V and the socket is for the standard continental Europlug (type C and F). Visitors bringing electrical devices from the UK will need a continental adaptor plug. American appliances will need a transformer.

Preceding pages **Narrow street in Gamla Stan**

Left **Road signage** Right **Passengers waiting at Stockholm Central Station**

TOP 10 Getting There

1 Arlanda Airport
This is Sweden's major international airport, and is located 37 km (23 miles) north of Stockholm. Direct flights operate to a wide range of European destinations and North America. Terminals 2 and 5 serve international flights; domestic flights depart from 3 and 4. ⊗ *www.arlanda.se/en*

2 From the Airport
The Arlanda Express airport train will whisk you to the city centre in 20 minutes. The airport coach services take around 40 minutes. Taxis will go to any city centre destination for a fixed fee. ⊗ *www.arlandaexpress.com/start.aspx*

3 Bromma Airport
Located just 7 km (5 miles) northwest of downtown Stockholm, Bromma Airport can be easily reached by airport coach, local bus, or taxi. Flights are limited due to environmental restrictions, but there is a regular service to Brussels and numerous domestic destinations. ⊗ *www.brommaairport.se/en/Bromma/Traveller*

4 Skavsta Airport
Situated near Nyköping, 100 km (62 miles) south of Stockholm, Skavsta is Sweden's major airport for low-cost carriers, and caters to many European destinations. Access to Stockholm is by an 80–90 minute airport coach service. Alternatively, take a train from Nyköping. ⊗ *www.skavsta.se/en*

5 Västerås Airport
Close to Västerås city, 110 km (68 miles) south-west of Stockholm, this tiny airport terminal mainly serves flights to London. Stockholm can be reached by a 80–90 minute airport coach service, or by train from Västerås. ⊗ *www.stockholmvasteras.se*

6 By Train
Stockholm Central Station is the main rail hub for both intercity and local rail services. Visitors arriving from elsewhere in Europe can avail the daily express services, every two hours, to and from Copenhagen. You can also take the train from Copenhagen to Malmö and then the overnight sleeper service.

7 Swedish Railways
The state-owned railway operator Statens Järnvägar (SJ), runs most intercity routes, though there are some private train operators. SJ's X2000 high-speed trains connect the major cities. The lowest fares can be purchased 90 days in advance. Suburban commuter trains are run by the local transport authority, Storstockholms Lokaltrafik (SL). SL travel cards and tickets are valid on these services. ⊗ *www.sj.se*

8 By Boat
There are ferries from Finland (Helsinki and Turku), Estonia (Tallinn) and Latvia (Riga) to Stockholm. Take a ferry from Poland (Gdansk) to Nynäshamn, 60 km (37 miles) south of Stockholm. ⊗ *Tallink Silja Line: 08 666 33 30; www.tallinksilja.com • Viking Line: 08 452 40 00; www.vikingline.se*

9 By Coach
Eurolines has direct coaches from Central Europe to Stockholm, but they are unlikely to be cheaper than a budget flight or a rail ticket. Swebus is the main domestic coach operator, and its network extends to Norway, Denmark, Germany and the Czech Republic. ⊗ *Eurolines: www.eurolines.se • Swebus: 02 002 182 18; www.swebusexpress.se*

10 By Car
The Öresund toll bridge connects Denmark and Sweden. The toll is around 375 kr for a passenger vehicle. Then follow the E4, a 550-km (340-mile) continuous motorway to Stockholm. A congestion tax is levied on vehicles within central Stockholm, and parking can be expensive.

Flygbussarna provides coach services to Stockholm from all of the airports – www.flygbussarna.se/

Left **Stockholm tram** Centre **Traffic signs on a street** Right **Passengers waiting to board a ferryboat**

Top 10 Getting Around

1 Tickets

All SL tickets are valid for travel on the underground, bus, tram or local train, and can be used for combined journeys. While single tickets are valid for unlimited journeys in a one-hour period, a strip of multiple tickets, called a *remsa*, offers better value. However, 24-hour, 72-hour, weekly and monthly passes offer the best deal for regular travel, and cover the Djurgården ferries and trams. *www.sl.se*

2 Tunnelbana

The regular and efficient underground is the fastest way to get around town. It has three lines – red, green and blue. Trains run until around midnight on weekdays, and all night on Fridays, Saturdays and the night before most public holidays.

3 By Bus

Stockholm has an extensive bus network. While most services operate until around midnight, some major routes run all night. There are night bus services seven days a week to many destinations further afield.

4 By Tram

The tram network, largely dismantled in 1967, has recently made a comeback. Line 7N, between the city centre and Waldemarsudde, preserved as a heritage route, has re-opened to regular traffic. You can still take a vintage tram from spring to autumn, and SL passes (but not tickets) are valid on them.

5 By Local Train

Local trains are cheap and handy for several destinations further afield. The pendeltåg (local train) extends from the port of Nynäshamn, 60 km (37 miles) south of the city, to Märsta near Arlanda Airport. The Saltsjöbanan suburban rail provides an easy connection between the city and Saltsjöbaden, while the narrow-gauge Roslagsbanan serves 39 destinations northeast of the city.

6 By Boat

Mostly operated by Waxholmsbolaget, boats provide a vital link to several islands in the archipelago, as well as sights in Lake Mälaren. Services in summer are more frequent; check the timetables carefully. You can travel on the daily Djurgården ferries from Slussen (SL pass valid) in just 10 minutes. *www.waxholmsbolaget.se*

7 Taxis

Taxi Stockholm, Top Cab, Taxi 020 and Taxi Kurir are some reputable companies, and their vehicles are never far away in the city centre. However, these taxis are expensive – a trip from a suburb to the city centre may cost around 300 kr; a short hop across the city will rarely be under 150 kr. *Taxi 020: www.taxi020.se • Taxi Stockholm: www.taxistockholm.se • Taxi Kurir: www.taxikurir.se • Top Cab: www.topcab.com*

8 Walking

Walking is a great way to explore Stockholm. The city has wide pavements and walking distances between many metro stations are relatively short. Vehicles are obliged to stop at road crossings. Paths along quaysides, in parks and along esplanades are shared with cyclists; be sure to stay on the pedestrian side.

9 By Car

Driving in the centre is not encouraged; parking is expensive and difficult to find. There are 25 park and ride stops on the way to central Stockholm to encourage usage of public transport. Sweden has very tough drinking and driving laws.

10 Cycling

Although it is easy to pedal in the city through its network of bike lanes, the going can get tough in winter. Hire bikes for three days or for a season at Stockholm City Bikes from April to October. *www.citybikes.se*

Stockholm Public Transport runs 365 days a year, with a slightly reduced service at Christmas, Midsummer and on New Year's Day.

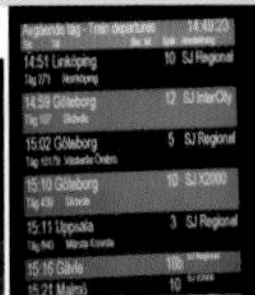

Left **Tourist information office** Centre **Electronic Train timetable** Right **A Swedish daily**

Top 10 Useful Information

1 Tourist Information

The main tourist office is on Vasagatan, across the street from Stockholm Central Station. Large and modern, it is well stocked with guides, maps and leaflets about the city and further afield. Visitors can book accommodation and guided tours here. *Vasagatan 14 • Map L3 • 08 508 285 08 • Open 9am–6pm Mon–Fri, till 7pm in summer, 9am–4pm Sat, 10am–4pm Sun*

2 Internet Sites

Sweden's official website for travel and tourist information is multilingual, as is the Stockholm Tourist Center's website. A great introduction to Sweden in English is www.sweden.se, the official gateway to Sweden, packed with tourist and general information. *Stockholm Tourist Center: www.visitstockholm.com • Sweden's official website: www.visitsweden.com*

3 Maps

You will need an up-to-date and easily navigable map to find your way around the city. When planning your trip, www.hitta.se is a great online map resource for locating any address. The tourist centre stocks free maps of the city and its surroundings. The transport information offices sell an excellent, detailed map. *www.stockholmmap.se*

4 What's On

Published monthly by the Stockholm Visitors Board and available free at the city tourist office, this pocket-sized guide provides information on latest events such as music festivals, sports and exhibitions. It also includes maps. *www.stockholmtown.com*

5 Transport Information

Stockholm Local Transport has excellent information online in English, including a journey planner. Customer care services are also available in English 24 hours a day. Some travel centres provide timetables for all transport routes. *Stockholm Local Transport: www.sl.se/en/Visitor/Plan-your-journey • Customer Service: 08 600 10 00*

6 Radio Sweden International

You can catch up on the latest news on Sweden year-round with English broadcasts on *Radio Sweden International*. Half-hour broadcasts are at 8:30pm Swedish time, Monday to Friday on 89.6MHz. *www.sverigesradio.se*

7 Swedish Newspapers

The main national newspapers, *Dagens Nyheter, Svenska Dagbladet, Aftonbladet* and *Expressen*, all have event listings, or you can pick up the *Metro Stockholm* newspaper for free from stands at all underground stations.

8 International Newspapers

The larger Pressbyrån stores, particularly in the city centre, have a very good stock of international newspapers, often the same day's publication. Head to the store in Stockholm Central Station for the best selection. Prices are not cheap – expect to pay around 25 kr for a slimmed-down international version.

9 Sightseeing Tours

Strömma offers well-organised sightseeing tours on buses and boats. You can acquaint yourself with the city on a 75-minute bus tour. Boat trips range from a quick 50-minute cruise through the central canals to extensive tours through the archipelago. *www.stromma.se/en*

10 Gay and Lesbian Travellers

You will find news, useful tips and guides on the website of Stockholm Gay & Lesbian Network, which is part of Stockholm Visitors Board. For more information on what's on, go to www.qx.se. *www.stockholm-gay-lesbian-network.com*

Storytours (www.storytours.eu) is excellent for walking tours in the Old Town.

Left **Stockholm taxi** Centre **Beggar on the street** Right **Pub counter**

TOP 10 Things to Avoid

1 Overpriced Taxis
Taxis are expensive, but in Stockholm's unregulated market, some small licensed firms can charge outrageous prices. Never take an unlicensed taxi – licensed ones have yellow licence plates. Stick to Taxi Stockholm, TopCab, Taxi Kurir and Taxi 020.

2 Drottninggatan
The southern end of Drottninggatan is full of tacky tourist shops and forgettable restaurants, preying on tourists who drift there from Gamla Stan. The street improves to the north, and beyond Kungsgatan (as you go towards Vasastan), it gets pleasant with good shops, cafés and restaurants.

3 Single Travel Tickets
The fare system for local transport favours regular travellers but there are good options for those on a shorter stay *(see p106)*. A single ticket for the central zone costs 36 kr, even if it is for just a two-minute journey between two metro or bus stops. Unless you only intend to use public transport for one or two trips, pick up a pass or discount ticket strip to suit your stay.

4 Beggars
Begging in Stockholm is a rare sight and many who ply this trade – often on local trains with cards detailing fictitious stories – are controlled by gangs. Do not give anything as it does not help their plight. Stockholm's Stadsmission is the official charity for the homeless, with some excellent shops around town. *www.stadsmissionen.se*

5 Drugs
Sweden has a zero-tolerance policy towards all controlled drugs, including cannabis. Penalties range from fines for possession of a small amount of cannabis up to 10 years in prison for more serious offences.

6 Buying a Round of Drinks
Alcoholic drinks in bars are generally expensive and there is no real custom of buying rounds of drinks in Sweden.It is not at all rude to simply buy your own drinks during the evening when in a group. If you offer to buy drinks for Swedes they may just think you are a generous foreigner, so do not expect to receive one in return.

7 Bottled Water
Tap water in Stockholm and throughout Sweden is of very high quality and there is no need to buy expensive bottled water. In cafés, bars and restaurants, tap water is always offered and often available in jugs. If you ask for water with a meal, it should come from the tap.

8 Tea in Cafés
Tea often costs as much as a cappuccino or latte – 30 kr or higher – but do not expect it to be served in a fancy china pot. Often you will be handed a glass or cup and left to prepare the tea yourself from a supply of teabags and hot water. At home, however, Swedes prefer to brew loose tea, and tea shops across Stockholm sell many specialist mixtures.

9 Casinos in Bars and Nightclubs
Some bars and nightclubs have low-stakes blackjack tables with rules – the dealer wins all tied hands – absurdly in favour of the house. For more responsible gaming, go to the state-run Casino Cosmopol. Security rules require all guests to be registered and photographed.
Kungsgatan 65
• *www.casinocosmopol.se*

10 Rogue Door Staff
All nightclubs have door staff – the majority are professional and helpful. However, a small minority have been known to refuse admission for no reason or to force patrons to leave. If you encounter a problem, walk away – they will not change their mind. Call or write a complaint to the management later.

Travelling on public transport without a valid ticket risks a fine of 1,200 kr.

Left **Backpackers waiting on the roadside** Right **Picnicking in the park**

Top 10 Stockholm on a Budget

1 Walking

It is not just that Stockholm is pedestrian-friendly – walking is the best way to discover the city's beauty. The city centre is compact, pavements are wide and well maintained and pedestrian crossings are to be found on both major and minor roads. Further afield, countryside walks are aplenty and the public enjoys *allemansrätt* – the freedom to roam.

2 Dagens Lunch

If you thought that eating out in Stockholm was expensive, then think again. Do as the locals and make *Dagens rätt* (lunch of the day) your main meal. Served even in some more upmarket establishments Monday through Friday, it includes a main course, salad, soft drink and tea/coffee, all for around 70–100 kr. No wonder that most office workers take a full hour for a sit-down meal.

3 Public Transport

An SL period pass is good value – but you can also use it on some great day trips. The medieval town of Sigtuna, 50 km (31 miles) north of Stockholm, takes about an hour by train and bus. If you want to visit the archipelago by bus, take Bus 428X from Slussen to Björkviks Brygga, which takes about an hour. *www.sl.se*

4 Museums for Free

Some museums offer free entry on some mid-week evenings at certain times of the year – check with the tourist office for the latest details. The Stockholm Card *(Stockholmskortet)* provides free entry to more than 80 museums. *www.stockholm.se/stadshuset*

5 Drinking In

With prohibitive drinking prices in most bars, follow the Swedish tradition of *förfest*, or pre-party, and have a drink before going out. Prices in the state monopoly Systembolaget are reasonable, and it has an excellent selection of beers, wines and spirits from around the world. It closes at 6pm Monday to Friday, on Saturday afternoon and on Sunday.

6 Drinking Out

You can drink out for surprisingly good prices – you just have to know where to look. The quest for cheap beer invariably leads to more rough-and-ready haunts. Carmen, near Medborgarplatsen, attracts a friendly mix of students, musicians and novelists. *Carmen: Tjärhovsgatan 14 • Map D5 • 08 641 2412*

7 Picnics

Spoilt for choice when it comes to parks, locals do not hesitate to get picnic baskets in warmer weather. Tantolunden, near Hornstull, Rålambshovsparken, on Kungsholmen, and Djurgården are some of the popular bigger parks. Note that some parks, particularly those near residential areas, have restrictions on drinking alcohol.

8 Clubbing for Free

Nightclubbing does not have to mean waiting in a long queue only to part with a big wad of cash before your first drink. Two of Debaser's clubs, one at Slussen and the other at Medborgarplatsen, frequently offer free entry before 10pm on Fridays and Saturdays, often with hip and happening live bands followed by DJs until 3am. *www.debaser.se*

9 Sightseeing on a Budget

Board Tram 7 from Sergels Torg, or a vintage tram from Norrmalmstorg, to Waldermarsudde. The scenic route runs past the elegant mansions on the waterfront of Strandvägen and on to the beautiful parkland of Djurgården.

10 Churches

Stockholm's excellent selection of churches *(see pp56–7)* are all free and sometimes host concerts – particularly around the time of religious festivals.

Most hotel rates are exclusive of breakfast – but if you pay extra, expect a hearty buffet breakfast with a wide choice of dishes.

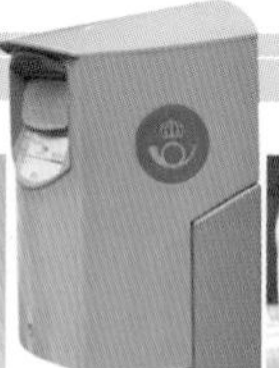

Left **Money exchange sign** Centre **Local postbox** Right **People withdrawing money from ATMs**

Top 10 Banking and Communications

1 Money

Sweden's currency is the krona (SEK or kr, plural kronor). The krona is divided into 100 öre. Coins are 1, 5 and 10 kr. Banknotes come in 20, 50, 100, 500 and the rarer 1,000 kr. Do not worry about making a small payment to break a 500 kr note; it is common. Many stores price goods in krona and the smaller öre, such as 19.95 kr, even though öre coins are no longer in circulation. The total cost of your shopping is rounded off to the nearest krona.

2 Banks

Most banks are open from 9:30am or 10am until 3pm, Monday to Friday. You may need to give advance notice if you want to make a cash withdrawal of more than 10,000 kr. Major banks include Handelsbanken, SEB and Swedbank.
www.handelsbanken.se • www.seb.se • www.swedbank.se

3 Money Exchange

There are several bureaux de change in downtown Stockholm, including at the central rail and coach stations. Otherwise, it is possible to withdraw krona from an ATM with your bank or credit card – check with your bank for the charges it levies. Some ATMs at Arlanda Airport dispense euros and even UK pounds.

4 ATMs

Cash machines are reasonably common in the city centre but a little harder to find elsewhere. Almost all banks have one, usually located outside the premises. Sometimes you may find that only 500 kr notes are available.

5 Credit Cards

Credit cards are accepted almost anywhere, with Chip and PIN terminals in nearly all establishments. For some transactions, particularly larger ones including money exchange, you may be asked to show some form of ID.

6 Payphones

With mobile phone ownership considered the norm for almost everyone in Sweden, payphones are nearing extinction. In spite of that, you will still find a fair number dotted around the city – most accept 10 kr coins or phonecards that you can get from Pressbyrån or 7/11 stores.

7 Mobile Phones

Mobile phone reception is good throughout the city, even on the underground rail system. Etiquette about usage is fairly relaxed; use commonsense and you will be fine. You might invite huge roaming fees with your home operator if you have an unlocked phone; buying a local operator's pay-as-you-go SIM card and some credit is always an option.

8 Post Offices

The national post office, Posten, has leased most of its counter operations to private shops – look out for the blue and yellow Posten symbol outside news agencies or supermarkets. You can buy stamps at Pressbyrån or 7/11 stores. Post is efficient but expensive. Postboxes are yellow for national and international mail; blue for those with the Stockholm postcode areas (100–199). Latest collections are usually at around 5pm to 6pm and 4pm for further afield.

9 Internet

Most homes in Stockholm have high-speed Internet so cafés never really caught on. However, many Pressbyrån stores have Internet terminals for hire. Wi-Fi access is available almost everywhere, including hotels.

10 Pressbyrån

Pressbyrån is your one-stop shop for daily essentials, newspapers and magazines, coffee and buns, travel tickets, stamps, Internet, phone and SIM cards. The stores are located at most underground and railway stations and on several high streets.

To find your nearest Pressbyrån store, visit www.pressbyran.se

Left **City Dental's signboard** Centre **Luggage lockers at the station** Right **Lifesaver at quayside**

TOP 10 Security and Health

1 Emergencies

Call 112 from any phone for all emergency services; it will work regardless of whether or not you have international roaming or phone credit. All operators speak English and interpretation services are also available.

2 Hospitals

Swedish hospitals are excellent. You must have a valid European Health Insurance Card if you are from the EU/EES, or else you have to pay the fees yourself. Visitors from other countries should make sure they have some form of health insurance.

3 Doctors

If you have a European Health Insurance Card when visiting a doctor, you pay the same fee as residents – around 160 kr per visit. Sweden has agreements with certain countries regarding fees; visit www.vardguiden.se for full details. *City Akuten, Apelbergsgatan 48 • Map L2 • Open 8am–6pm Mon–Fri • No prior appointments required • General health advice: 08 32 01 00*

4 Dentists

If you desperately need a dentist, City Dental, in the city centre, is open seven days a week, with dentists speaking around 40 different languages. You will have to pay a fee. *Drottninggatan 27 • Map L2 • 08 200 680 • www.citydental.se*

5 Pharmacies

In 2009, the lifting of government monopoly on pharmaceutical sales led to the emergence of many private pharmacies. Nevertheless, regulations governing the sales of pharmaceuticals in Sweden remain strict; a prescription is often required to purchase medicines that can be bought over the counter in many other countries. *Apotek C.W. Scheele, Klarabergsgatan 64 • Map L3 • 07 714 504 50 • Open 24 hours • www.apoteket.se*

6 Crossing the Road

Swedes tend to be well behaved regarding pedestrian crossings with traffic lights, so do not be surprised to see people waiting patiently for the green signal even if there is no car in sight. At crossroads with lights, even though you have the right to cross when the signal is green, traffic is still allowed to turn in when pedestrians are not crossing. This can be a little unnerving, but you have the right of way. Always look out for cyclists when crossing.

7 Police

You can contact the police in a non-emergency at 114 14. You should report crimes such as theft for insurance purposes – you will then be provided with the necessary documentation. The police are friendly and helpful and most of them speak English. Visitors can feel free to ask them any questions without any hesitation.

8 Crime

Stockholm is generally a very safe city, and no precautions are necessary except common sense. Pickpockets are the greatest hazard; always keep your valuables safe, as brazen attempts at theft in crowded bars are not uncommon.

9 Women Travellers

With a strong emphasis on sexual equality, women should feel comfortable in Sweden. Unwelcome attention is rare, and if so, usually from harmless drunks. Apply common sense precautions late at night.

10 Gay and Lesbian Travellers

Sweden is considered to be one of the most gay-friendly countries in the world. Homosexuality has been legal since 1944 and the age of consent was equalized in 1972. The Swedish parliament voted to make same-sex marriages legal in 2009 by an overwhelming majority of 261 to 22.

The city centre police station is at Kungsholmsgatan 43.

Left **Radisson Blu Waterfront Hotel** Centre **Hotel Diplomat** Right **Nobis Hotel**

Top 10 Luxury Hotels

1 Grand Hotel

Sweden's top five-star hotel has a great location by the waterfront. This luxurious hotel also boasts the Michelin-starred Mathias Dahlgren restaurants and the Cadier Bar, renowned for its extraordinary drinks selection. *Södra Blasieholmshammen 8 • Map N4 • 08 679 35 00 • www.grandhotel.se* • ⓀⓀⓀⓀ

2 Nobis Hotel

The emphasis at this contemporary luxury hotel is on timeless style and optimum function. In the heart of the city, it features an Italian-style restaurant and bistro, plus the super-cool Gold Bar and Lounge. *Norrmalmstorg 2–4 • Map M2 • 08 614 10 00 • www.nobishotel.se* • ⓀⓀⓀ

3 First Hotel Reisen

With its wonderful waterside setting near the Royal Palace, the Reisen is a classic hotel with a maritime theme. Standard rooms have views of the Old Town while the superior rooms look out across the waterfront and luxury rooms boast private saunas, Jacuzzis and balconies. *Skeppsbron 12 • Map N5 • 08 22 32 60 • www.firsthotels.com/reisen* • ⓀⓀⓀⓀ

4 Radisson Blu Waterfront Hotel

A modern hotel close to the Stockholm Central Station, the Waterfront Hotel is connected to the 3,000 seater Stockholm Waterfront Congress Centre, and is popular for major business functions. Its rooms offer excellent views. *Nils Ericssons Plan 4 • Map K4 • 08 505 060 00 • www.radissonblu.com* • ⓀⓀⓀⓀⓀ

5 Clarion Sign

This city centre hotel reflects the Scandinavian spirit in its classic furniture and black and white photographs. The Clarion Sign also features a spa, with a heated outdoor pool, gym and sauna, all with fantastic views across Stockholm. *Östra Järnvägsgatan 35 • Map K3 • 08 676 98 00 • www.clarionsign.com* • ⓀⓀⓀ

6 Elite Eden Park Hotel

Close to Stureplan's nightlife district, this hotel has an English-style gastropub. There are 124 comfortable rooms, a gymnasium and a sauna. *Sturegatan 22 • Map N1 • 08 555 627 00 • www.elite.se/eng/edenpark* • ⓀⓀⓀⓀ

7 Berns Hotel

A boutique hotel, Berns is right in the city centre and an ideal choice for those interested in the city's nightlife. The hotel's 2.35:1 nightclub features world-famous and top Swedish DJs. *Nackströmsgatan 8 • Map M3 • 08 566 32 00 • www.berns.se* • ⓀⓀⓀⓀ

8 Hotel Rival

The brainchild of ABBA legend Benny Andersson, Rival is one of the coolest places to stay in Stockholm. Situated by leafy Mariatorget square in the lively Södermalm district, Rival hosts regular DJ events in its stylish bar, and the restaurant has a lovely outdoor summer terrace. *Mariatorget 3 • Map C5 • 08 545 789 00 • www.rival.se* • ⓀⓀⓀⓀ

9 Scandic Grand Central

Housed in a 130-year-old building, Scandic Grand Central is centrally located close to the railway station and Arlanda Express. The Acoustic Bar features live music, and there is a great-value lunch buffet during the week, popular with workers from the nearby offices. *Kungsgatan 70 • Map K2 • 08 512 520 00 • www.scandichotels.com* • ⓀⓀⓀ

10 Hotel Diplomat

A classical hotel in the heart of an exclusive part of Stockholm, the Diplomat offers lovely views over the water to nearby Djurgården, with vintage tramcars passing by along Strandvägen in the summer. The refurbished T/BAR is a trendy spot to relax in the evening. *Strandvägen 7c • Map P3 • 08 459 68 00 • www.diplomathotel.com* • ⓀⓀⓀ

Wi-Fi access is usually available in all hotels.

Interior of Rex Hotel

Price Categories

For a standard double room and taxes per night during the high season. Breakfast is not included, unless specified.

Ⓚ under 1000 kr
ⓀⓀ 1,000–1,500 kr
ⓀⓀⓀ 1,500–2,000 kr
ⓀⓀⓀⓀ 2,000–2,500 kr
ⓀⓀⓀⓀⓀ over 2,500 kr

Top 10 Mid-Range Hotels

1 Park Inn by Radisson Hammarby Sjöstad Hotel

This hotel offers modern conveniences in one of Stockholm's newer neighbourhoods, the eco-friendly Sjöstaden. A skip across the canal by boat, then bus, takes you to the centre. *Midskeppsgatan 6 • 08 506 886 00 • www.parkinn.com* • ⓀⓀⓀ

2 Elite Hotel Arcadia

This comfortable hotel is in a quiet residential area, but the Tekniska Högskolan underground provides quick links to the centre. It is also a short stroll to the bars and restaurants of Vasastan. Arcadia also has apartments with kitchenettes for longer stays. *Körsbärsvägen 1 • Map D1 • 08 566 215 00 • www.elite.se* • ⓀⓀⓀ

3 Rex Hotel

A homely and friendly hotel in a refurbished town house dating from 1866, the Rex has brick walls and colourful furnishings. Only a block away from Sveavägen, it is in an area with a host of restaurants and bars. *Luntmakargatan 73 • Map C2 • 08 16 00 40 • www.rexhotel.se* • ⓀⓀ

4 Pärlan Hotell

Meaning "the pearl", this hotel is exactly that, with nine cosy and affordable rooms in a building that was once a school for girls. Furnished in warm, old-fashioned style, it is located on a quiet side street in the chic Östermalm district. *Skeppargatan 27 • Map P2 • 08 663 50 70 • www.parlanhotell.com* • ⓀⓀⓀⓀ

5 Central Hotel

In an excellent location almost opposite the main railway station and ideal for arrivals from all airports, the comfortable Central Hotel is renowned for its friendly welcome. It is an affordable option in the heart of the city. *Vasagatan 38 • Map K2 • 08 566 208 00 • www.profilhotels.com* • ⓀⓀⓀ

6 Adlon Hotel

Dating from the 19th century, the Adlon's exterior evokes the style of the 1950s, but offers all modern facilities. In a busy location close to the city shops, it is also handy for the coach arrivals from the airports. *Vasagatan 42 • Map K2 • 08 402 65 00 • www.adlon.se* • ⓀⓀ

7 Hotel Esplanade

With a grand frontage facing the water on Strandvägen, Hotel Esplanade reflects the Art Nouveau style of its 1910 origins. Tastefully renovated and upgraded through the years, this family hotel still retains many of its original features. It is in a very handy spot both for Djurgården and Stureplan's restaurants and nightlife. *Strandvägen 7a • Map N3 • 08 663 07 40 • www.hotelesplanade.se* • ⓀⓀⓀⓀ

8 August Strindberg Hotell

A lovely little garden where you can enjoy breakfast in summer is the highlight of the August Strindberg. The hotel is tucked away on a quiet side street just off the most interesting part of Drottninggatan and is perfect for the downtown shops. *Tegnergatan 38 • Map J1 • 08 32 50 06 • www.hotellstrindberg.se* • ⓀⓀⓀ

9 Rica Hotel Gamla Stan

The perfect choice to make the most of the Old Town experience, the Rica Gamla Stan is housed in a charming 17th-century building full of atmosphere. The terrace is a little oasis, and the hotel is close to the Gamla Stan station. *Lilla Nygatan 25 • Map M5 • 08 723 72 50 • www.rica-hotels.com* • ⓀⓀⓀ

10 Scandic Sjöfartshotellet

This Södermalm hotel's hidden gem is the summer rooftop bar with great views out to the archipelago and an intimate atmosphere. The room rates include access to the gym and breakfast. *Katarinavägen 26 • Map D5 • 08 517 349 00 • www.scandichotels.com* • ⓀⓀⓀ

Unless otherwise stated, all hotels accept credit cards.

Left **Façade, Hotel Bema** Centre **Hotel Micro's reception** Right **Interesting signage of Tre Små Rum**

TOP 10 Budget Hotels

1 Hotel Tre Små Rum

This is a superb value option in a convenient location in Södermalm, close to the underground and local train stations. The rooms are cosy and breakfast is included in the price.
Högbergsgatan 81 • Map C5 • 08 641 23 71 • www.tresmarum.se • Kr

2 Connect Hotel City

This hotel is quite basic in its approach, with some very small rooms – but offers good rates for its location in the heart of the liveliest part of Kungsholmen. There is an early booking discount.
Alströmergatan 41 • Map A2 • 08 441 02 20 • www.connecthotel.se • Kr

3 Hotel Zinkensdamm

Situated in Tantolunden park on Södermalm, Hotel Zinkensdamm includes breakfast and Internet access in its price; it has a bar too. It is both a hotel and hostel, and is a pleasant place to stay. *Zinkens Väg 20 • Map B5 • 08 616 81 10 • www.hotellzinkensdamm.com* • Kr Kr Kr

4 Hotel Bema

Facing the Tegnerlunden park and with an indoor courtyard garden, Hotel Bema has a pleasant location, right in the city. It is a good choice for anyone looking for a central hotel at a fair price.
Upplandsgatan 13 • Map C2 • 08 23 26 75 • www.hotelbema.se • Kr Kr

5 Hotel Micro

The theme of this hotel is small rooms at small prices. The rooms are windowless and bathroom facilities shared, but if your aim is to explore the city and you want a central place to sleep, it offers a genuine budget price.
Tegnerlunden 8 • Map C2 • 08 545 455 69 • www.hotelmicro.net • Kr

6 Hotel Anno 1647

Situated in two former houses from the 17th and 18th centuries, Anno is on a side street just off Götgatan, one of Södermalm's main shopping and bar streets. It is just a few steps away from the Slussen underground and bus station, making for excellent transport links.
Mariagränd 3 • Map D5 • 08 442 16 80 • www.anno1647.se • Kr Kr Kr

7 Formule 1 Stockholm Syd

This chain of hotels is all about sleeping well at the lowest prices. Rooms are simple with toilets and bathrooms along the corridor. It is a 10-minute walk to the Telefonplan underground, with regular trains into the city, which run until well after midnight and even later on weekends.
Mikrofonvägen 30 • 08 744 20 44 • www.hotelformule1.com • Kr

8 Hotel Attaché

Out of town in a quiet residential area, Attaché has 60 rooms in varying sizes to choose from and breakfast is included in the room prices. The trendy Landet bar and restaurant is nearby if you want to stay in the neighbourhood.
Cedergrensvägen 16 • 08 18 11 85 • www.hotelattache.se • Kr Kr

9 Quality Hotel Nacka

This hotel has 162 rooms comfortable rooms, a restaurant plus a pool and sauna. In summer, visitors can enjoy a meal or drink on the beautiful terrace. There is free parking just outside the entrance.
Värmdövägen 84 • 08 506 160 00 • www.choicehotels.no • Kr Kr

10 2Kronor Hotel City

Located very close to the shopping street, Drottninggtan, the 2Kronor Hotel City has large rooms with high ceilings and mullioned windows. Choose between rooms with private baths or shared facilities.
Kammakargatan 62 • Map K1 • 08 796 96 00 • www.2kronorhotel.se • Kr Kr

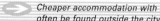

Cheaper accommodation with good public transport links can often be found outside the city centre.

Interior of the Guldgränd Hotel Apartments

Price Categories

For a standard double room and taxes per night during the high season. Breakfast is not included, unless specified.

Ⓚ	under 1000 kr
ⓀⓀ	1,000–1,500 kr
ⓀⓀⓀ	1,500–2,000 kr
ⓀⓀⓀⓀ	2,000–2,500 kr
ⓀⓀⓀⓀⓀ	over 2,500 kr

Top 10 B&Bs, Hostels and Apartments

1 Hostel af Chapman

Stay in a 19th-century ship on Skeppsholmen, overlooking the Royal Palace and near many of the city's museums. There are beds in shared cabins starting from 260 kr per person, or a private one from 590 kr. *Flaggmansvägen 8 • Map P5 • 08 463 22 66 • www.svenskaturistforeningen.se* • Ⓚ

2 Lunda Pensionat

On a pleasant street not far from the Zinkensdamm underground, Lunda has double rooms with views over Lake Mälaren and the City. It also has ship-cabin style rooms. There is a fully equipped kitchen and access to computers. *Lundagatan 31 • Map B5 • 07 364 357 69 • www.lundapensionat.se* • Ⓚ

3 Rygerfjord Hotel and Hostel

A former Norwegian ferry boat, this has been converted into a hotel and hostel while retaining its nautical feel. Some rooms overlook Lake Mälaren with fine views across to the City Hall. *Södermälarstrand, Kajplats 12–14 • Map C4 • 08 84 08 30 • www.rygerfjord.se* • Ⓚ

4 City Backpackers Inn

This classic hostel with lots of character and even free pasta, has excellent security, free Internet, laundry, a guest kitchen and very helpful staff. There is a variety of rooms to choose from. *Upplandsgatan 2a • Map K2 • 08 20 69 20 • www.citybackpackers.org* • Ⓚ

5 Bed & Breakfast 4trappor

On the fourth floor of a residential building close to hip SoFo on Södermalm, this apartment has both a bedroom and living room, a kitchen and bathroom and is stylishly decorated. *Gotlandsgatan 78 • Map D6 • 08 642 31 04 • www.4trappor.se* • Ⓚ

6 Globen Bed and Breakfast

Live like a local in a typical Swedish wooden house in a residential part of Stockholm near Globen and its underground station. There is a fully equipped cottage as well as a studio. It has a garden and friendly dogs are welcome. *Dammtrappgatan 13 • 07 367 980 60 • www.globenvilla.se* • Ⓚ

7 Bed & Breakfast Stockholm at Mariatorget

These modern apartments are in the same building as the entrance to the Mariatorget underground. There are two apartments for one or two persons, or both can be booked to accommodate three or four people; there is a connecting door. *Torkel Knutssonsgatan 35 • Map C5 • 07 057 972 00 • www.bedbreakfast-stockholm.com* • Ⓚ

8 Stockholm Hostel

This air-conditioned hostel is in Kungsholmen district, a five-minute ride on the underground from Stockholm Central station. Each room has a private bathroom. Guests can prepare their own meals in the two communal kitchens. *Alströmergatan 15 • Map A2 • 07 015 655 25 • www.stockholmhostel.se* • Ⓚ

9 Guldgränd Hotel Apartments

In a 17th-century building close to the Slussen underground in a busy part of Södermalm, Guldgränd has spacious and stylish single, double and triple rooms as well as family apartments. *Guldgränd 5 • Map D5 • 08 641 40 64 • www.guldgrand.se* • Ⓚ

10 Biz Apartment Hotel

This hotel has 175 classy apartments; choose between one- and two-bedroom apartments or a range of studios ideal for the solo traveller. It has good deals for extended stays of weeks or months. *Sehlstedtsgatan 4 • 08 578 553 00 • www.bizapartmenthotel.se/gardet* • ⓀⓀ

Some small apartment accommodation and B&Bs do not accept credit cards.

Left **Scandic Anglais** Centre **The Red Boat Hotel** Right **Tea tray in Mornington Hotel**

TOP 10 Hotels with a Difference

1 Story Hotel

A quirky boutique hotel, this is a lively place with a touch of class. It has a "retro" modern restaurant, and DJs play music in the bar four nights a week. The hotel offers a variety of room types to choose from. *Riddargatan 6 • Map N2 • 08 545 039 40 • www.storyhotels.com* • Kr Kr Kr

2 Scandic Anglais

The buzz in this hotel is all about the music – DJs six nights a week. There are 230 standard rooms with wooden flooring. Dine in its restaurant or pick up a drink from one of its popular bars. A buffet breakfast is included in the rate. *Humlegårdsgatan 23 • Map M1 • 08 517 340 00 • www.anglais.se* • Kr Kr Kr

3 Långholmen Hotel and Youth Hostel

Staying in a prison cell may not be everyone's dream – but that is the unique appeal of this former jail, which saw its last prisoners in 1975. It is now a modern hotel and hostel on the central island of Långholmen. *Långholmsmuren 20 • Map A5 • 08 720 85 00 • www.langholmen.com* • Kr Kr

4 The Red Boat Hotel

A novel place to stay is on this boat moored quite close to the Old Town. There are actually two boats – a hotel and a hostel; the wooden-panelled cabins of the hotel are the cosiest. *Södermälarstrand Kajplats 10 • Map C4 • 08 644 43 85 • www.theredboat.com • Kr (hostel rooms) Kr Kr (hotel rooms)*

5 Jumbo Stay

If you have ever wished for your own private bedroom in an airplane, you can have just that on this converted 747 airliner at Arlanda Airport. It is truly a unique experience. *Jumbovägen 4, Arlanda Airport • 08 593 604 00 • www.jumbostay.com* • Kr Kr

6 Columbus Hotel

This atmospheric hotel was built in 1780 as a brewery, and later converted into barracks, a hospital and emergency rooms. It is located in the Södermalm area amidst the liveliest nightlife. *Tjärhovsgatan 11 • Map D5 • 08 503 112 00 • www.columbushotell.se* • Kr Kr

7 Clarion Hotel Stockholm

The hotel is in a residential part of Södermalm. You will not find many tourists here, but will not go short of eating and drinking options either. The cool upstairs bar in this hotel, with views across to Globen, is a popular meeting spot for Södermalm's media crowd. *Ringvägen 98 • Map D6 • 08 462 10 00 • www.clarionstockholm.com* • Kr Kr

8 Hotel Skeppsholmen

This hotel has earned rave reviews as one of the trendiest places to stay. It combines the atmosphere of a building from 1699 with classic modern design and is on a beautiful and peaceful city island with swift bus connections to the centre. *Gröna gången 1 • Map Q5 • 08 407 23 50 • www.hotelskeppsholmen.com* • Kr Kr Kr Kr Kr

9 Villa Källhagen

Located by the canal at Djurgården, Villa Källhagen is a peaceful place to stay within easy transport reach of the centre. To sit by an open window in its highly rated restaurant in the summer is truly idyllic. *Djurgårdsbrunnsvägen 10 • Map F3 • 08 665 03 00 • www.kallhagen.se* • Kr Kr Kr

10 Mornington Hotel

This charming boutique hotel is located in the heart of Östermalm. A library with 4,000 books is the outstanding feature of this place and it also has a secret patio garden in summer. *Nybrogatan 53 • Map N1 • 08 507 330 00 • www.mornington.se* • Kr Kr Kr

Many hotels have special offers, particularly in the low season, so it can pay to shop around.

Fish spas at Yasuragi Hasseludden

Price Categories

For a standard double room and taxes per night during the high season. Breakfast is not included, unless specified.

Ⓚ	under 1000 kr
ⓀⓀ	1,000–1,500 kr
ⓀⓀⓀ	1,500–2,000 kr
ⓀⓀⓀⓀ	2,000–2,500 kr
ⓀⓀⓀⓀⓀ	over 2,500 kr

Top 10 Out-of-town Accommodation

1 Hotel J

By the waters of the inner archipelago with connections to the city by boat, Hotel J has a New England nautical theme (wicker, blue and white). It is a great summer destination to unwind and has a popular restaurant. *Ellensviksvägen 1, Nacka Strand • 08 601 30 00 • www.hotelj.com • ⓀⓀ*

2 Stallmästaregården Hotel

A former coaching inn from the 1700s, this hotel, located very close to Hagaparken, overlooks the lake. Although further afield, it is still a reasonable walk or a very short bus journey to bars and restaurants around Odenplan. *Norrtull • 08 610 13 00 • www.stallmastaregarden.se • ⓀⓀⓀ*

3 Ibis Stockholm Hägersten

Located on the southern approach to Stockholm, near the furniture retailer IKEA, this hotel offers high standards at reasonable prices. Friendly, multi-lingual staff makes this hotel a popular choice. *Vastertorpsvägen 131 • 08 556 323 30 • www.ibishotel.se • Ⓚ*

4 Kastellet Bed & Breakfast

In the ancient fort of Vaxholm, this B&B is a good base for exploring the archipelago. Most of the archipelago ferries out of central Stockholm stop at the town of Vaxholm and from there you can reach some of the beautiful islands by boat in a short time. *Vaxholms Kastell, Vaxholm • 08 541 330 35 • www.kastelletbnb.se • ⓀⓀ*

5 Åtellet Hotel

This is a modern hotel built in the style of a 19th-century merchant house that reflects the character of the small town of Norrtälje at the time. The hotel has waterside views and serves very good value lunches on weekdays. *Sjötullsgatan 10, Norrtälje • 01 767 004 50 • www.atellet.se • ⓀⓀⓀ*

6 Yasuragi Hasseludden

Yasuragi is the Japanese word for inner peace and harmony, and this unusual spa hotel offers a variety of rejuvenating treatments. There is a tranquil Japanese garden stretching down to the water and two restaurants serving Asian cuisine. *Hamndalsvägen 6, Saltsjö-Boo • 08 747 64 00 • www.yasuragi.se • ⓀⓀⓀ*

7 Clarion Hotel Gillet

Its location in central Uppsala makes this chic design hotel a good base to explore the city. Clarion Hotel Gillet has modern rooms and a trendy atmosphere, with music nights in the bar. *Dragarbrunnsgatan 23, Uppsala • 01 868 18 00 • www.clarionhotelgillet.com • ⓀⓀ*

8 Grinda Inn Hotel

An old farm house set among fields and with an atmospheric summer harbour café-bar, this hotel allows you to make the most of Grinda island's simple charm. *Grinda (archipelago) • 08 542 494 91 • www.grinda.se • Ⓚ*

9 Grand Hotel Saltsjöbaden

Inspired by the Hôtel de Paris in Monte Carlo, this is a majestic hotel. Located by an archipelago harbour, Grand Hotel Saltsjöbaden is just 25 minutes by a quaint train to Slussen. The hotel often offers some good-value deals. *Hotellvägen 1, Saltsjöbaden • 08 506 170 00 • www.grandsaltsjobaden.se • ⓀⓀⓀ*

10 Sigtuna Stads Hotell

This is Sweden's smallest five-star hotel. Dating from 1909, Sigtuna Stads Hotell has been tastefully restored to retain its original elegance. In summer you can eat dinner overlooking the waters of Sigtunaviken. *Stora Nygatan 3, Sigtuna • 08 592 501 00 • www.sigtunastadshotell.se • ⓀⓀⓀⓀ*

Several hotels have a lunch set menu on weekdays.

General Index

Page numbers in **bold** type refer to main entries. The Swedish letters å, ä and ö fall at the end of the alphabet.

Acknowledgments

The Author
Paul Eade was born and raised in Scarborough, England, but has lived in Stockholm since 1999. He has some Swedish favourites: *julmust*, the short but sweet summer, and Swedish indie pop. A lover of cricket himself, Paul is on an ongoing mission to introduce the noble sport of cricket to Swedes. He enjoys travelling, particularly in Germany.

Photographer James Tye

Additional Photography
Peter Hanneberg; Frits Solvang; Erik Svensson; Jeppe Wikstrom

Special Assistance

Johan Tegel at Stockholm Visitors Board (SVB)

Fact Checker Kathleen Sauret

At DK INDIA

Managing Editor
MadhuMadhavi Singh

Senior Editorial Manager Savitha Kumar

Senior Design Manager Priyanka Thakur

Project Editor Bidisha Srivastava

Editor Gayatri Mishra

Project Designer Vinita Venugopal

Designer Deepika Verma

Assistant Cartographic Manager
Suresh Kumar

Cartographer Mohammad Hassan

Picture Research Manager Taiyaba Khatoon

Assistant Picture Researcher
Lokesh Bisht

DTP Designer Rakesh Pal

Indexer Helen Peters

Proofreader Indira Chowfin

At DK LONDON

Publisher Vivien Antwi

List Manager Christine Stroyan

Senior Managing Art Editor
Mabel Chan

Senior Editor Sadie Smith

Project Editor Vicki Allen

Designer Tracy Smith

Senior Cartographic Manager
Casper Morris

Picture Research Assistant Marta Bescos Sanchez

Senior DTP Designer Jason Little

Production Controller Kerry Howie

Picture Credits
Placement Key: a-above; b-below/bottom; c-centre; f-far; l-left; r-right; t-top

Photography Permissions
Dorling Kindersley would like to thank the following for their assistance and kind permission to photograph at their establishments:

Adolf Fredriks Kyrka; Åhléns City; Akademibokhandeln; Aquaria Vattenmuseum; Arkitekturemuseet; BluVelvet; Byredo; B.A.R.; Café Vuma; Centralbadet; Cloud Nine Food & Cocktails; Drottningholm; F12; Jens Hollingby at Fotografiska; Gina Tricot; Golden Hits; Gondolen; Grill; Kicki Kollstedt at Gröna Lund; Gudrun Sjödén; Gustav Vasa Kyrka; Hagaparken; Siv Falk at Historiska Museet; Jenny Helldahl at Junibacken; Kaffe; Konditori Ritorno; Kungliga Opera; Kvarnen; Leksaksmuseet; Maria Magdalena Kyrka; Mellqvist Kaffebar; Randy Jämtlid at Millesgarden; Hans Riben at Musik & Teatermuseet; Anders Svensson at Nordiska Museet; Nytroget Urban Deli; Observatoriemuseet; Oliver; Östermalms Ostasiatiska Museet; Pizza Hatt; Riddarholmskyrkan; The

Royal Palace (Kungliga Slottet); Saluhall; Saturnus; SF Bokhandeln; Skansen; Helene Winberg at SoFo; Spårvägsmuseet; Stadsbiblioteket; Stadshuset; Storkyrkan; Strand; Strindbergsmuseet; Sturecompagniet; Sturegallerian; Teatergrillen; Tjabba Thai; Tom Tits Experiment Museum; Twist; Tyska Kyrkan; Ulla Winbladh; Urban Outfitters; Vapiano Gamla Stan; Martina Siegrist Larsson at Vasamuseet; Vete-Katten; WeSC.

Works of art have been reproduced with the permission of the following copyright holders:

© Millesgården: *Europe and the Bull*, 1926 35tl; *Poseidon*, 1930 99cla; *Six Angels Musicians*, 1949–1950 99cla; *Civilian and Policeman* #2 © Liu Bolin 34bl.

The publisher would like to thank the following for their kind permission to reproduce their photographs:

ALAMY: Maria Grazia Casella 80–81; Chad Ehlers 110tr; Peter Forsberg 54bl; InterFoto 32tl.
CADIER BAR, GRAND HOTEL STOCKHOLM: 48tr, 88tl.
CORBIS: Macduff Everton 12–13; Grand Tour/Maurizio 44–45; Johner Images/Marten Adolfson 14tr; Catherine Karnow 13cb; Henrik Trygg 15tl.
DREAMSTIME.COM: Irakite 96cr; Alessandro Rizzolli 13cl; Birgitta Sjöstedt 14tl.
FOTOLIA: dusk 97br; fransos66 6clb; Igor Groshev 12cla.
GETTY IMAGES: AFP/Sven Nackstrand 39tl; Archive Photos/ Transcendental Graphics 32tr; Hulton Archive 32bc; The Image Bank/Tariq Dajani 13bl; Johner Images/Jeppe Wikstram 30–31; Look/Jan Greune 102–103; Photographer's Choice/ Chad Ehlers 15c,/Slow Images 1c; Anders Sellin 12cb.
GRÖNA LUND: 23bl.
HOTEL NOBIS, NORRMALMSTORG: Louise Billgert 112tr.
KAKEN: Mathias Nordgren 48tl.
MASTERFILE: Siephoto 13tl
MISTRAL: Erik Olsson 101tl.
POPAGANDAFESTIVAL: Victor Lundmark 38tl.
RADISSON BLU WATERFRONT HOTEL: 112tl.
REX HOTEL: 113tl.
THE SPY BAR: 50bl.
HISTORISKA MUSEET: 26c, 27c; Christer Åhlin 26cla, 26crb, 26-27c, 27tl, 27bl; Sören Hallgren 26bc; Gabriel Hildebrand 27clb.
STOCKHOLM CULTURAL FESTIVAL: Karin Nilsson 38tr.
STOCKHOLM INTERNATIONAL HORSE SHOW: Roland Thunholm 38br.
STOCKHOLMS ÖL & VIN AB: Örs Gubas 39br.
STOCKHOLM SKÄRGÅRDSSTUGOR AB: 14bl.
VASAMUSEET, STOCKHOLM: Hans Hammarskiöld 11clb.
YASURAGI HASSELUDDEN: 117tl.

Phrase Book

When reading the imitated pronunciation, stress the part which is underlined. Pronounce each syllable as if it formed part of an English word, and you will be understood sufficiently well. Remember the points below, and your pronunciation will be even closer to the correct Swedish.

Guidelines for Pronunciation

ai:	as in 'fair' or 'stair'
ea:	as in 'ear' or 'hear'
ew:	like the sound in 'dew'
EW:	try to say 'ee' with your lips rounded
oo:	as in 'book' or 'soot'
OO:	as in 'spoon' or 'groom'
r:	should be strongly pronounced

Swedish Alphabetical Order

In the list below we have followed the Swedish alphabetical order. The following letters are listed after z: **å, ä, ö**.

In an Emergency

Help!	**Hjälp!**	yelp
Stop!	**Stanna!**	stanna!
Call a doctor!	**Ring efter en doktor!**	ring efter ehn doktor
Call an ambulance!	**Ring efter en ambulans!**	ring efter ehn ambewlanss
Call the police!	**Ring polisen!**	ring poleesen
Call the fire brigade!	**Ring efter brandkåren!**	ring efter brandkawren
Where is the nearest telephone?	**Var finns närmaste telefon?**	vahr finnss nairmasteh telefawn
Where is the nearest hospital?	**Var finns närmaste sjukhus?**	vahr finnss nairmasteh shewkhews

Communication Essentials

Yes	**Ja**	yah
No	**Nej**	nay
Please (offering)	**Varsågod**	vahrshawgOOd
Thank you	**Tack**	tack
Excuse me	**Ursäkta**	ewrshekta
Hello	**Hej**	hay
Goodbye	**Hej då/adjö**	haydaw/ahyur
Good night	**God natt**	goonutt
Morning	**Morgon**	morron
Afternoon	**Eftermiddag**	eftermiddahg
Evening	**Kväll**	kvell
Yesterday	**Igår**	ee gawr
Today	**Idag**	ee dahg
Tomorrow	**I morgon**	ee morron
Here	**Här**	hair
There	**Där**	dair
What?	**Vad?**	vah
When?	**När?**	nair
Why?	**Varför?**	vahrfurr
Where?	**Var?**	vahr

Useful Phrases

How are you?	**Hur mår du?**	hewr mawr dew
Very well, thank you.	**Mycket bra, tack.**	mewkeh brah, tack
Pleased to meet you.	**Trevligt att träffas.**	treavlit att traiffas
See you soon.	**Vi ses snart.**	vee seas snahrt
That's fine.	**Det går bra.**	dea gawr brah
Where is/are …?	**Var finns …?**	vahr finnss…
How far is it to …?	**Hur långt är det till**	hewr lawngt ea dea till
Which way to …?	**Hur kommer jag till …?**	hewr kommer yah till …
Do you speak English?	**Talar du/ni engelska?**	tahlar dew/nee engelska
I don't understand	**Jag förstår inte**	yah furshtawr inteh
Could you speak more slowly, please?	**Kan du/ni tala lång-sammare, tack.**	kan dew/nee tahla lawng-ssamareh tack
I'm sorry.	**Förlåt.**	furrlawt

Useful Words

big	**stor**	stOOr
small	**liten**	leeten
hot	**varm**	varrm
cold	**kall**	kall
good	**bra**	brah
bad	**dålig**	dawleeg
enough	**tillräcklig**	tillraikleeg
open	**öppen**	urpen
closed	**stängd**	staingd
left	**vänster**	vainster
right	**höger**	hurger
straight on	**rakt fram**	rahkt fram
near	**nära**	naira
far	**långt**	lawngt
up/over	**upp/över**	ewp/urver
down/under	**ner/under**	near/ewnder
early	**tidig**	teedee
late	**sen**	sehn
entrance	**ingång**	ingawng
exit	**utgång**	ewtgawng
toilet	**toalett**	too-alett
more	**mer**	mehr
less	**mindre**	meendre

Shopping

How much is this?	**Hur mycket kostar den här?**	hewr mewkeh kostar dehn hair
I would like …	**Jag skulle vilja…**	yah skewleh vilya
Do you have?	**Har du/ni …?**	hahr dew/nee …
I'm just looking	**Jag ser mig bara omkring**	yah sear may bahra omkring
Do you take credit cards?	**Tar du/ni kreditkort?**	tahr dew/nee kredeetkoort
What time do you open?	**När öppnar ni?**	nair urpnar nee
What time do you close?	**När stänger ni?**	nair stainger nee
expensive	**dyr**	dewr
cheap	**billig**	billig
size (clothes)	**storlek**	stOOrlek
white	**vit**	veet
black	**svart**	svart
red	**röd**	rurd
yellow	**gul**	gewl
green	**grön**	grurn
blue	**blå**	blaw
antique shop	**antikaffär**	anteek-affair
bakery	**bageri**	bahgeree
bank	**bank**	bank
book shop	**bokhandel**	bOOkhandel
cake shop	**konditori**	konditoree
chemist	**apotek**	apoteak
market	**marknad**	marrknad
newsagent	**tidningskiosk**	teednings-cheeosk
post office	**postkontor**	posstkontOOr
supermarket	**snabbköp**	snabbchurp
tobacconist's	**tobakshandel**	tOObaks-handel
travel agency	**resebyrå**	reasseh-bewraw

There are two words for 'you': 'du' (familiar form) and 'ni' (polite form). It is not impolite to address a complete stranger with the familiar form.

Sightseeing

art gallery	**konstgalleri**	konnst-galleree
church	**kyrka**	chewrka
garden	**trädgård**	traidgawrd
house	**hus**	hews
library	**bibliotek**	beebleeotek
museum	**museum**	mewseum
square	**torg**	tohrj
street	**gata**	gahta
tourist information office	**turist-informations-kontor**	tureest-informashOOns kontOOr
town hall	**stadshus**	statshews
closed for holiday	**stängt för semester**	staingt furr semester
bus station	**busstation**	bewss-stashOOn
railway station	**järnvägsstation**	yairnvaigsstashOOn

Staying in a Hotel

Do you have any vacancies?	**Har ni några lediga rum?**	hahr nee negra leadiga rewm
double room with double bed	**dubbelrum med dubbelsäng**	doobelrewm med doobel seng
twin room	**dubbelrum med två sängar**	doobelrewm med tvaw sengar
single room	**enkelrum**	enkelrewm
room with a bath	**rum med bad**	rewm med bahd
shower	**dusch**	dewsh
key	**nyckel**	newckel
I have a reservation	**Jag har beställt rum**	yah hahr bestellt rewm

Eating Out

Have you got a table for...	**Har ni ett bord för...?**	hahr nee ett bOOrd furr ...
I would like to reserve a table.	**Jag skulle vilja boka ett bord.**	yah skewleh vilya bOOka ett bOOrd
The bill, please.	**Notan, tack.**	nOOtan, tack
I am a vegetarian	**Jag är vegetarian**	yah air vegetariahn
waitress	**servitris**	sairvitreess
waiter	**servitör**	sairviturr
menu	**meny/ matsedel**	menew/ mahtseadel
fixed-price menu	**meny med fast pris**	menew med fast prees
wine list	**vinlista**	veenlista
glass of water	**ett glas vatten**	ett glahss vatten
glass of wine	**ett glas vin**	ett glahss veen
bottle	**flaska**	flaska
knife	**kniv**	k-neev
fork	**gaffel**	gaffel
spoon	**sked**	shead
breakfast	**frukost**	frewkost
lunch	**lunch**	lewnch
dinner	**middag**	middahg
main course	**huvudrätt**	hewvewdrett
starter	**förrätt**	furrett
dish of the day	**dagens rätt**	dahgens rett
coffee	**kaffe**	kaffeh

Menu Decoder

apelsin	appelseen	orange
bakelse	bahkelse	cake, pastry, tart
banan	banahn	banana
biff	biff	beef
bröd	brurd	bread
bullar	bewllar	buns
choklad	shooklahd	chocolate
citron	sitrOOn	lemon
dessert	dessair	dessert
fisk	fisk	fish
fläsk	flaisk	pork
forell	fooraill	trout
frukt	fruckt	fruit
glass	glass	ice cream
hummer	hummer	lobster
kallskuret	kall-skuret	cold meat
korv	koorv	sausages
kyckling	chewkling	chicken
kött	churtt	meat
lamm	lamm	lamb
lök	lurk	onion
mineralvatten	minerahl-vatten	mineral water
mjölk	m-yurlk	milk
nötkött	nurtchurtt	beef
ost	oost	cheese
olja	olya	oil
potatis	potahtis	potatoes
ris	rees	rice
rostat bröd	rostat brurd	toast
räkor	raikoor	prawns
rött vin	rurtt veen	red wine
saft	safft-	lemonade
sill	seell	herring
skaldjur	skahl-yewr	seafood
smör	smurr	butter
stekt	stehkt	fried
salt	sallt	salt
socker	socker	sugar
soppa	soppa	soup
sås	saws	sauce
te	tea	tea
torr	torr	dry
ungsstekt	ewngs-stehkt	baked, roast
vispgrädde	veesp-graiddeh	whipped cream
vitlök	veet-lurk	garlic
vitt vin	veett veen	white wine
ägg	aigg	egg
äpple	aippleh	apple
öl	url	beer

Numbers

0	**noll**	noll
1	**ett**	ett
2	**två**	tvaw
3	**tre**	trea
4	**fyra**	flewra
5	**fem**	fem
6	**sex**	sex
7	**sju**	shew
8	**åtta**	otta
9	**nio**	nee-oo
10	**tio**	tee-oo
100	**(ett) hundra**	(ett) hewndra
200	**tvåhundra**	tvawhewndra
300	**trehundra**	treahewndra
400	**fyrahundra**	fewrahewndra
500	**femhundra**	femhewndra
1 000	**(ett) tusen**	(ett) tewssen

Time

one minute	**en minut**	ehn meenewt
one hour	**en timme**	ehn timmeh
half an hour	**en halvtimme**	ehn halvtimmeh
ten past one	**tio över ett**	teeoo urver ett
quarter past one	**kvart över ett**	kvahrt urver ett
half past one	**halv två**	halv tvaw
two o'clock	**klockan två**	klockan tvaw
13.00	**klockan tretton**	klockan tretton
16.30	**sexton och trettio**	sexton ock tretti
noon	**klockan tolv**	klockan tolv
midnight	**midnatt**	meednatt
Monday	**måndag**	mawndahg
Tuesday	**tisdag**	teesdahg
Wednesday	**onsdag**	oonssdahg
Thursday	**torsdag**	toorsdahg
Friday	**fredag**	freadahg
Saturday	**lördag**	lurrdahg
Sunday	**söndag**	surndahg

Selected Street Index